WIDE OPEN WRITING

praise for *Wide Open Writing*

"If you are in any way interested in writing; if you are in any way interested in diving deep; if you are in any way interested in connection and a rich learning experience, then book yourself on a Wide Open Writing retreat. The way that Dulcie and Nancy create and hold space for you to explore your writing on a whole new level is really something very special. A WOW retreat is SO MUCH MORE than a writing retreat, it will tend to your body, mind and soul. Transformational can be an over-used word… but not in this case, and you should be warned…they can be life changing! If you're reading this you might be thinking about signing up for one, all I can say is - go on, treat yourself, you won't be disappointed."
— *Vikki Smisek*

"There's nothing more valuable for a writer, or those of us who dream of writing, than to give yourself the gift of time, in a beautiful place, with expert and caring stewards, to discover the raw material of your stories: yourself."
— *Michael Schaefer*

"When I signed up for the WOW retreat in Tuscany last year, I had just lost my beloved husband of 34 years, endured trauma surgery after a serious fall, and was braced for a cloud of locusts to land on my lawn. For months on end, I felt desperate to break out of the paralysis of grief and injury. I had been writing a novel for a couple of years and wanted to renew the urge to finish it, maybe discover some ideas for some short stories. But what I really dreamed about finding in Tuscany was the inspiration to start a new chapter in my own life. Maybe even a whole new book. I wasn't disappointed. The heartfelt collaboration between Dulcie and Nancy and among my "sisterhood of strangers" against the backdrop of the Tuscan hills generated a powerful buzz of creative energy that still vibrates in my soul. So whether you're looking for purely creative inspiration or deep spiritual healing or a combination of both, as I was, just open your heart. Chances are you'll find more than you thought possible."
— *Sharon MaHarry*

"I got a group experience that I craved, with fabulous women, some of whom I know and love very much, and others that I wanted to meet very much."
—*Curry Ander*

"Dulcie brings both firm ground and the possibility to reach the moon to her teaching. She penetrates the surface and plumbs the depth until you're not sure what hit you, but you know she got you. She is a warrior for the written word and the hungry heart."
—*Jodi Paloni*

"I wasn't sure what to expect when I submitted two short stories to Nikki for editing and feedback. What she gave me for the price of a consultation was above and beyond what I'd anticipated I would receive. Nikki is a post-apocalyptic fiction writer and I have more of a Southern-quirk sensibility, so I wasn't entirely sure how she would approach my work. The feedback was of significant value to me in ways I'd not anticipated. As it turns out, working with someone outside of my genre offered great benefits (never underestimate the power of a different point of view). Not only did she edit my work for style, she was also so generous with content ideas. If you tell a story well, Nikki will help you tell it better. I think that is because she loves words - writing them, reading them, weaving them, and spinning them into something magical. What meant the most to me, though, was actually meeting with Nikki to receive her feedback directly and seeing her genuine enthusiasm for my stories. I think I am a better writer because of the editing services I solicited from Nikki and am excited to continue working with her."
—*Laurin Bellg*

Wide Open Writing:
Embrace Your Creative Genius

Nancy Coleman
and the
Wide Open Writing team

WOW Rising Press
an imprint of Minerva Rising Press

Copyright © 2021 Nancy Coleman
All rights reserved. No part of this book may be reproduced in any form or by any electronic or mechanical means, including information storage and retrieval systems, without permission in writing from the publisher, except by reviewers who may quote brief passages in a review.

ISBN 978-1-950811-08-3

Cover Photo by Nancy Coleman
Book design by Brooke Schultz

Printed and bound in USA
First Printing May 2021

Published by WOW Rising Press
16 Twin Pond Road
Topsham, Maine
04086

To the Muse of all writers, awakened in Tuscany, alive in every one of us.

"Who wants to become a writer? And why? Because it's the answer to everything… It's the streaming reason for living."

— Enid Bagnold

CONTENTS

Introduction	1
1: Origins	3
2: Getting Ready, Getting Started	7
3: The Retreat Begins	11
4: Ritual	17
5: Practice	25
6: Inspiration	29
7: Silence	35
8: Vision	39
9: Positivity	47
10: Voice	51
11: At Home in the Body	57
12: Heart	63
13: Play	69
14: Getting (What's in the Way) Out of the Way	75

15: Connection and Support	85
16: Manifestation and Celebration	91
Appendix A: More Prompts	97
Appendix B: More Readings	98
Appendix C: Sample Wide Open Writing Retreat Schedules	100
Acknowledgements	105
About the Author	107

INTRODUCTION

"You are your own new frontier."

— Julia Cameron

Welcome.

The journey you are about to take marks a new beginning. Wherever you are in your writing life, the fact that you've picked up this book signals a threshold that lies before you. You've opened these pages because you heard a quiet call, a whisper of untold stories. You wanted more from your writing, from your life. You felt called to go on a writing retreat and you aren't able to do that right now. However you have come to this place, right here, right now; please take a moment. Pause to notice how this threshold feels to you.

In the center of all of our daily lives live potent but largely hidden possibilities. For many of us, these possibilities lie dormant, pressed out of sight by every other kind of demand in our busy and responsible lives. We come to disbelieve in the presence or the worth of our whispered urgings toward *more*. It's easier, in a way, to follow well-traveled roads.

But more is entirely possible. The path to *more* is wide open if you know how to traverse it. You can find in the center of your daily life places of solitary wonder, even ecstasy, in which to cultivate the creative energy you seek. You can come to sense your deep and enduring connection with creative beings all over the world as you connect strongly with yourself. The contemplative and sacred curiosity you develop can become a habit and you can come to know and love yourself as the writer you already are.

Writing is a path to the creative genius in all of us, and open creative expression is a saving grace in the world. Wide Open Writing wants to help you get from where you are to where you most want to be as a writer and a person. Positivity and expansiveness, the cornerstones of our work and the most important tools in a creative toolkit, will give you access to your essential creative channels and simultaneously make you a better writer. That is a promise.

Nothing quite compares to the wide open spaces of a creative life. Nothing measures up to the luxury of getting away from daily life to recharge batteries, to open new channels of creativity, to nourish the muse in evocative landscapes and in profound connection with other writers. What is in store for you in this book is the invitation to find and embrace that luxury *wherever you are*.

You're in good hands. Your hands. The hands who will write your way through the book. And ours, the hands of the many Wide Open Writing staff and alumni who offer up here everything we've learned about how to make a writing retreat for yourself that nourishes, excites, opens gateways, makes magic, and forms lasting connections. If this isn't the time to take a break from work or family, or it isn't the time to make any radical moves at all, perhaps it may yet be the ideal time to carve out of your circumstances the space you most need.

And so, this book.

Please stay tuned and stay curious. This is an invitation to your richest life.

1
Origins

"You do not have the see the entire staircase, you only have to take the first step."
— Martin Luther King, Jr.

    Wide Open Writing is a collective creativity community of writers who lead retreats and groups and online gatherings for writers at almost every step of the writing path. This book, a compendium of everything we've learned from our own writing years, is a collective effort. For ease of understanding, just one of us, Nancy Coleman, will be the narrator.

    Before we called ourselves writers, the Wide Open Writing team were mothers, journalists, corporate executives, professors, actors, psychologists, graphic designers, and yoga teachers, sometimes all at once. Each of us has a story about our beginnings: We wrote fairy tales as children; we wrote angst-filled poems about boyfriends and girlfriends; we wrote to try to understand pain and hold on to glory. But it takes more than any initial yearning or strong emotion to grow and sustain a writing life.

    After her first career forayed into chicken farming, wallpapering, and hotel management, Dulcie Witman worked as a family and substance abuse counselor for decades. When she wasn't "working," she quietly wrote stories long into the night. When the writer in her called out loudly enough that she had no choice but to obey, she enrolled in the Creative Writing MFA Program at Goddard College and has been writing and teaching ever since.

    Regina Tingle, an inspired and talented writer, led student groups in Europe for many years before she turned to the Goddard MFA program to move her writing and her life forward. At

Goddard, Dulcie and Regina found inspiration, built skills and, most importantly, found creative community. After graduate school ended and they returned to their lives in Maine and Italy, they began to trade emails and talk. They shared writing. They shared dreams. They tried to imagine how the creative fires they'd tended could continue to burn bright in their lives. And they had an idea.

    I am Dulcie's partner. At the same time as Dulcie was growing her creative writing life, I had been in private practice as a psychologist and a therapist for over thirty years. My own writing life grew in a grassroots way from the childhood memoir I had to write to get it out of my system. When I couldn't do any more with the memoir myself, I worked under the guidance of a brilliant development editor, Suzanne Kingsbury, who taught me how to turn scattered draft pages into polished product.

    By way of keeping inspiration alive, Regina showed pictures to Dulcie of a Tuscan farmhouse where she'd often taken college students on exchange programs in Italy. Dulcie showed Regina pictures of a coastal inn in Maine. Tuscany won: We decided we would invite friends and family and colleagues to join us on a writing retreat. In September of 2014, we gathered up a few fellow travelers, took off for the Italian farm, and a spark was lit. We wrote together for a week in idyllic surroundings, and the seeds of Wide Open Writing were born. The Tuscan agriturismo provided the ideal circumstances to dig into our writing. We discovered that everything we'd learned as therapists about healing, creativity, and growth was also powerfully applicable to the development and sustenance of a writing life.

The three of us came away from that first retreat with an idea for the future that grew as we grew and that took shape with all the influences each of us brought. We would gather our forces from academic training and work with editors. We would cull the best of our years as therapists and managers and group facilitators, as yoga teachers and meditators.

Yes, we wanted to travel, and we wanted to write, and writing together worked better than writing alone. But we also wanted to branch out from prevailing workshop models of teaching writing where critique was the primary tool. Instead, we would follow inklings and intuitions and emerging science to take our retreats in a direction that was more deliberately and defiantly positive and expansive. A participant in the first retreat suggested the name for this bold adventure, and the group became known as Wide Open Writing.

Like Dostoevsky, we've acted on the belief that "beauty will save the world." We wrote together in Tuscany and Mexico, Arizona and Maine, Morocco and Costa Rica. We imagined future retreats in Thailand and Finland and the Costa Brava in Spain. We learned how to do it, and we learned how to do it well; and somehow grace or magic walked alongside us everywhere we gave birth to these retreat experiences.

Then, in March 2020, in a matter of days, the world changed. Not only could we no longer travel to Tuscany, our original retreat home, but none of us could gather in groups of any kind anywhere in the world. What we might then have imagined would be a brief and inconvenient pause in business as usual became something more, lasting longer, going deeper, spreading wider for most of us than any single event in our lifetimes. Perhaps it would be a devastation. Perhaps it would be a threshold.

We were reminded that Shakespeare wrote both *King Lear* and *Macbeth* during the plague, and that Isaac Newton discovered the essential laws of gravity during the epidemic of his time. And while most of us hadn't yet produced masterpieces, maybe we could! Who knew what we would discover if we took creative time for ourselves?

We still wanted to write, and we could feel something about the original WOW inspiration evolving. We were called to create writing workshops not only by our restless spirits but by a longing in the world. In 2020, writers were on call to respond with new urgency and new awareness to what we were experiencing around us. Even before we couldn't go anywhere, we'd always known that Wide Open Writing wanted to connect with more people who'd felt the stirrings of stories within them.

Wide Open Writing has grown. Regina moved to England, started her own artist retreat business, and became a mother. Dulcie and I are joined now by a team of passionate and skilled volunteers and a modicum of paid helpers. During the COVID pandemic, we started an online membership option for writers who longed for on-going connection with creative community. We wrote this book. We raised funds to travel across North America in our new WOWMobile, where we would bring writing retreats to people who couldn't come to us. We aimed for *more*, as you are doing now. And *more* has come to fruition as we meet you now, in the pages of this book.

2
Getting Ready, Getting Started

"Whatever you can or dream you can, begin it..."
— Goethe

We've structured this book in the fashion of an in-person retreat in the original home of our first WOW getaway, a beautiful farm in the hills outside San Gimignano in Tuscany. Tuscany has become for Wide Open Writing participants and staff a symbol of the magic and the possibilities we've discovered together. We will refer to this countryside of ancient rolling hills throughout the book, because having a symbol, an imaginative place of connection, fosters creativity. It can be helpful to remember that even in our writerly isolation, we are not alone.

As you read through the pages of this book, we invite you to think of a place you love and to let the sense of that place accompany you in the exercises that follow. A deck by the sea. A mountain cabin. A chair under the pines in the backyard. Use our images from Tuscany, because that place holds the creative energy of hundreds of wide open writers, and add your own very particular sense of place, because this is your retreat.

Wide Open Writing, the book, is designed as an *experience* of what can happen when you make the time and space for your essential writer to emerge. The more thoroughly you engage with the chapters of this book, the more you'll get from the experience.

Every chapter contains at least one writing prompt. It will be best to try every one as you read along. Sometimes a beautiful notebook can encourage writing. Sometimes our inside voices demand expression so strongly that it doesn't matter how or where the words come out. However you do it, please do it.

The WOW Tuscan retreat begins on Sunday afternoon and ends on the following Friday, during which time we hold optional yoga practices every morning, twice-daily writing sessions, a mid-week afternoon off to explore and rest, a formal reading session, and a growing body of evening activities generated by the groups themselves. Your personal retreat may mirror ours, or may take a very different shape, the shape of your own life.

Retreat does not require international travel or new clothes for the journey. Retreat does not need fabulous vistas or delicious food fresh from the farm. These are marvelous addenda, no question. But the essential ingredients of retreats are simple ones: Space, privacy, and time.

SPACE and PRIVACY

"You do not need to leave your room...Remain sitting at your table and listen. Do not even listen, simply wait. Do not even wait, be quite still and solitary. The world will freely offer itself to you to be unmasked. It has no choice. It will roll in ecstasy at your feet."

— Franz Kafka

Space need not be spacious, but beauty helps. The WOW staff write in writing cabins, she-shacks, sitting in bed, at our desks, at the kitchen counter, in rehabbed closets and coffee shops, at a cousin's country cabin, on our yoga mats, at our altars.

Add a touch of inspiration: Photographs of a place you love or a writer you admire. A statue of an icon or a sacred teacher. Fresh flowers. A place for your eyes to rest when they're gathering thoughts.

Don't ask too much of your writing space. If it serves as office and playroom and writing studio, for instance, that may be more than you and the space can bear. Visual distractions and energetic cross-currents can clutter open spaces, and writers need open spaces.

Space requires privacy, even if that privacy is a corner of the studio apartment while wearing noise-canceling headphones. Please dedicate space that will be yours for the duration, even if that requires turning it back into a laundry room when you're done, even if that space is the back seat of your car. If you don't have to clear the area every time you sit down to write, that's ideal. A space that waits for you to arrive, a space to hold you while you're there, an area that remembers for you why you're there. Let the space take care of you.

For some of us, the sounds of other people are hopelessly distracting. For others, a general bustle in the background is soothing. If there's any way for you to deter interruptions during your writing time, please do. Make a sign or close a door or climb a tree, but make it clear. It's not forever, but it's essential.

What space will you carve out for your personal retreat?

At the same time, how will you connect with others? This is the other half of the writing life: Writers are as complicated as any group of humans. We work alone, and we need one another. How vital and yet how tender are our longings for connection with fellow writers. After we get over the appropriate initial anxieties, there's nothing quite so energizing as being able to show up authentically in a group of writers who are attempting to do the same. If you know someone with whom you could co-retreat either in person or via remote access, making that connection can be an excellent way to keep yourself moving forward with this work. Once several essential ground rules are in place, you can make great strides together. Chapter 9 has guidelines for the approach we take to giving and receiving feedback from ourselves as well as others. And if you don't know anyone with whom you'd like to share the process of this book, you might consider joining the Wide Open Writing Membership Group (https://wideopenwriting.com/), where we'd love to see you, hear your writing, and grow our writing lives together.

TIME

Retreat happens/In moments of insight/During planned time away/With awareness of Grace/Any minute, hour, day or week."

— Barbara Lindquist Miller

No perfect timing and no universally imperfect timing exist. No one way produces the best results for everyone. But we have suggestions as to how you might design your retreat on a timeline that suits you best:

- **The Full WOW:** Twelve chapters, twelve days, engaging with this book one chapter at a time, one day at a time, and filling out the days in a way that looks much like one of our Tuscany retreats, the schedule of which is listed in Appendix C. During a retreat, we mix things up. Yoga and morning writing; mid-day play and free-writing time; afternoon sessions to read and comment on each other's work. Your retreat might take a similar shape, in which you're committed to including a balance of writing and everything else that feeds and nourishes your life. You might schedule a massage or a hike or an Artist's Date (see Chapter 13) with yourself or arrange not to cook and do laundry during your time "away."

- **The Extended WOW**: Twelve chapters, twelve weeks. Spreading the retreat experience out over time is less immersive. If you like this approach to your Wide Open Writing retreat, or if this is just the way you need to do it, it will work best if you bring a daily writing practice along with you, using the days of each week to take yourself deeper into that week's prompts and inspirations. Given that it's more challenging to keep focus when you're planning a partial retreat than a full one, you'll want to read Chapters 4 and 5, Ritual and Practice, before you begin.

- **The Condensed WOW**: An in-between option and a fully immersive experience, the Condensed WOW combines reading and writing two chapters a day for five or six days. A condensed design might begin at the Beginning (evening 1), then move to a combination of Ritual and Inspiration

(Chapters 4 through 6), then Silence and Vision (Chapters 7 and 8), and so on through the sections.

- **Just the Prompts, Ma'am**: Although we've designed the book in an order corresponding to what you'd experience in a live in-person retreat, this is your book now. If you want to fly through the written part of the book, using it primarily as a book of prompts, the prompts in each chapter are easy to find. Go through the entire process or whether you make your own design for a retreat, you can always return to the listed prompts to try them again. Nancy and Dulcie have written pieces based on prompts in the book quite a few times and have found that every time there's still something new there. The memoirist Dani Shapiro says she's written the same memoir every decade of her life and somehow it comes out differently every time!

- **Make Your Own Retreat**: Whatever it takes. However you can. We encourage you to just. Do. It.

The chapters of this book are braided. Approximately every other chapter brings us experience and skill in how we move from *dream* to *manifestation*. We'll guide you in naming a *big dream* and we'll support you on your way there. These chapters are called *Inspiration, Vision, Voice, Heart, Getting Out of the Way, Connection and Support*, and *Manifestation and Celebration*. You will see that these processes are universal ones, the essential energies of any creative effort. Alternate chapters introduce the reader to Wide Open Writing's philosophy and practices. These chapters are called *Ritual, Practice, Silence, Positivity*, and *Life in the Body*, and are the ingredients we've culled to speak of WOW's particular magic.

However you've decided to come to the retreat, please make a commitment to yourself on that decision. Take those 45 minutes you have in the middle of your day. Take your twelve weeks of Saturdays or Tuesday evenings. Wake early and begin before the sun every day for a week. As is true of the space you're creating, time will take care of you once you claim it. And time unclaimed has a way of filling up instantly with miscellany. Be kind to yourself and be honest. Don't set yourself up for disappointment by promising yourself more than you can physically accomplish and at the same time, do make promises, ones you can keep.

> Over the years, I've found one rule. It is the only one I give on those occasions when I talk about writing. A simple rule. If you tell yourself you are going to be at your desk tomorrow, you are by that declaration asking your unconscious to prepare the material. You are, in effect, contracting to pick up such valuables at a given time. Count on me, you are saying to a few forces below: I will be there to write."
> — Norman Mailer

In the course of this book, we'll say more about the importance of dailiness and reliability. For now, it's interesting to reflect on a paradox at the heart of every creative journey: The wild and wide open portals to our creativity respond well to regularity and structure. Space and time. A place to land and a time to catch the muse as she flies.

Now, let's begin.

3
The Retreat Begins

> "All is in yourself
>   Things, thoughts, the stately
> shows of the world,
> the suns and moons,
> the landscape, summer
> and winter,
>   poems, endearments,
>   All."
> — Walt Whitman

September. Tuscany's afternoon lies still. A slight haze spreads across olive groves and vineyards in the wide patterned valley below where we sit. In the near distance, horses graze by a pond, the agriturismo walls glow a soft umber, and lavender scents the air. Under the pergola at the top of the hill, the chatter of our first words together fills the air and then subsides.

We have come from far away. Whether you've traveled to Italy or to the back bedroom, you've widened time and space into an opening for you to step through, for you to get away from what is everyday and distracting, for you to declare yourself to yourself. You seek a great beauty that will crack that rugged heart, that closed door you long to open. You hope to unburden the story you've been longing to tell. For any or all of these reasons that have brought you here, you are welcome.

We don't particularly like introductions as a way to begin a retreat. All of us know and perhaps dread those awkward statements we try to make at the start of group experiences, the ones that say why we are here and what we hope to gain from our experience. And so, we don't do them.

What we'll do is write. Because writing is what we came here to do, and, often, it is the thing we are most apprehensive about doing. Let's write.

> **Imagine this newly formed circle of writers, perhaps made up of friends or mentors, icons or idols, trusted allies. Imagine the Tuscan morning. For five minutes, please write down what you want these people to know about you.**

When you have taken five minutes, stop writing, set down your writing instrument, and read what you've written out loud. Pause to feel what you feel, to notice what you notice. Did you notice your responses to the words you've written? Were there words or phrases that pleased you, that displeased you? Did you imagine reactions from this imagined group to your writing? Did you think of things you wish you'd said?

Quickly write down or underline words or phrases that caught your eye or caught in your throat.

> **Now, for five minutes, please write down what you don't want these people to know about you.**

When you have taken five minutes, please read what you've written aloud. Pause to feel, notice, and then jot down reactions from within and from the imagined group to your words.

Pause again. Let yourself notice that everyone else in the group – and in this case, all of your fellow Wide Open Writers – has just shared with you the same courageous exercise of seeing within and expressing what is true, despite any natural resistance.

That's how the retreat begins. We invite you into this exercise in sharing what is light and what is shadow within you, because this is an essential starting point of creativity. We take it as a given that we all want to be seen, and that we are all afraid to be seen. It's a tender truth, really, that not every outpouring of our essential beings has been met with praise. Not one of us has arrived in our adult bodies without injury. We need one another, and we are afraid of one another. That's a starting point for our work together, not an end-point: Along with every other courageous Wide Open writer, you will practice bowing to the guardians and stepping across thresholds of trepidation. It gets easier,

and it gets wildly more interesting.

Now and then in a Wide Open Writing retreat, a participant decides not to read aloud what they've written. It's understandable. In one of our first retreats, I wrote, "I'm not as nice as you think I am." Reading it aloud was both challenging - in saying these words, I detonated a piece of my habitual identity - and at the same time, it felt immensely freeing. I found I could be quite a bit nicer, in fact, when loosed from the requirement to seem so. And I found I could use those words as a jumping off point for letting the spicier, fiercer inner voices speak out. Creativity loves freedom.

Inspiration from Others

Evening falls softly around our group at the top of the hill by the olive grove. As light turns golden, the scent of lavender is felt on the air. It's almost time to close our first session.

> **Please look for something that inspires you; a quote or a poem or a line, an essay or a story. Read that inspirational piece out loud, perhaps as you walk, and then reread it. Taste the syllables, the rhythm, feel the words on your skin.**
> **What is it that so inspires you about this piece?**
> **What is it that inspires you to come on this writing retreat at this moment?**
> **What is it that inspires you?**
> **Write for 10 minutes in reply to these questions.**

Imagine that your words are shared now in our newly formed circle. Imagine the feeling of inspiration shared.

> "A hunch is creativity trying to tell you something."
> — Frank Capra

People will say that writing is one percent inspiration and ninety-nine percent perspiration. But oh, that one percent! Without it, technique, persistence, craft, and cleverness might lend their help to grocery lists, to quick emails, to stories on the surface of your life. Without inspiration, it is likely that these stories will not fully satisfy you.

It's a good thing to practice craft games. There are many ways to become a more technically skilled writer, some of which we'll touch on in the course of this book. Once inspiration has given you the spirit of the work, it's still important to get better at your art. Practice is essential. You could stop reading right here and devote yourself to a daily writing practice, and that could become enough.

But what if you could practice writing with a deeper connection to your essential aliveness? The poet Mary Oliver asks, "Tell me, what is it you plan to do with your one wild and precious life?" *That's* what we're about. We want to generate access in each of us to those internal fountains of inspiration that bring us alive.

Consider this:

What am I doing here? What is the great work of my life? What puts the wind beneath my wings?

You don't have to have an answer. Raising the question can be enough. Posing the question while walking or showering or sitting in meditation or driving or writing will keep it alive. And as Rilke suggested to his young protege, "The point is to live everything. *Live* the questions now. Perhaps you will then gradually, without noticing it, live along some distant day into the answer."

With the longing that comes from inspiration, and even without any particular craft skills, you will still have a story that matters. You will, at the very least, have created the great block of stone from which your inner Michelangelo can begin to sculpt. If you're fortunate, you may open the channel of inspiration wide enough that a poem, a story, a song, slides through unhindered and emerges as a perfect being. Most likely, you'll find in the block of stone you've just created something of liveliness, an effervescent phrase, a thread of truth, something that resonates for you with a deep chord of recognition: Oh, that's what I'm talking about, you'll say. And then you can begin to perspire happily in the work of re-vision.

For now, let your questions sit lightly on your mind. We'll come back to them with some practices for living toward answers.

At this, the close of our first writing day, please devote a few minutes to quiet reflection.

Reward yourself in a way that's meaningful to you. Know that this matters. You're shaping your new relationship with your creative self, who will reward you thousands of times over for your kind attention.

In the first moments of a retreat or a writing project, it's important that we create a balance for excited but apprehensive nerves. In order for creativity to be sustainable and regenerative, every writer needs to form strong neural connections between the intense, exciting, work of writing and a palpable sense of support and ease. We need to learn in a visceral way that writing can be delicious and fun.

This is generally not taught or even experienced, but it is true. Because it isn't taught in formal ways, most creative people blunder our own ways toward relief from the intensity of the work. In that pursuit, many of us have tried just about anything without necessarily knowing what we're aiming for. Alcohol. Drugs. Sex. Procrastination. Shopping. Naps in the writing studio. Forays in nature. Yoga on the living room floor. Some approaches are more sustainable and less costly than others. But however it is achieved, overworked nervous systems need to learn that it's okay to be vulnerable. It's okay to be brave. It's okay to venture into territory that is unknown and perhaps dangerous. We want you to come to know that you will reliably emerge on the other side, that you can create a writing life in which your vulnerability is met with support, even with joy. The importance of this can't be over-emphasized.

This would be a perfect time to create the first of your own writing ritual practices at home.

4
Ritual

For me things and tasks that have a ritual to them are easier to get done. I shower and I know exactly which limb I start with when I dry myself, because it's the same one every morning. I know when I write, because it's the same hour every day. When I cook, I cut the onion in the exact same way every single time. My body knows what to do, so there's no time for my head to interfere with thoughts like 'Why aren't we watching Netflix?' or 'We should just stay in bed all day.'"

— Eline van Wieren

Human beings are custom-made for ritual.

From any perspective, from scientific to sacred, from the anthropological to the deeply personal, we recognize the ever-present importance of ritual for our human lives. Psychologists have been late to understand this — the first review article about the psychological significance of ritual wasn't published until 2017[1] — but the evidence there is clear too: Rituals help us regulate emotion while supporting us in moving toward our goals more effectively at the same time as they create and sustain important social connections.

How long does it take you on a visit to a new city to find "your" coffee shop, "your" best bakery? How long has it been since you've done something out of the ordinary on a weekday morning or eaten something very different for your first meal of the day? No matter how flexible you know

---

1 (The Psychology of Rituals: An Integrative Review and Process-Based Framework, Nicholas M. Hobson, Juliana Schroeder, Jane L. Risen, JSPP, 2017)

yourself to be, we humans are hard-wired to establish habits, which the cerebellum happily tucks away outside of consciousness so that we don't have to spend all our time considering just what it takes to stand up or walk or drive a car. So that we don't have to ask ourselves every morning what beverage we would like to have and how we'll prepare it. Habits make space for what we would rather be doing or thinking.

By comparison, ritual is habit *made intentional*. And rituals, or intentional practices, can help us move toward who and how we want to be. Rituals can set us free.

Think of the rituals already in place in your life. How do you take your morning beverage? What do you do before you leave the house? What kinds of evening or sleep habits do you have? What practices have you already created around your writing?

Writing and Ritual

Make a list of your writing rituals.

When he's writing a novel, Haruki Murakami wakes at 4:00 am and works for five to six hours straight. In the afternoons, he runs or swims or both, runs errands, reads, and listens to music; bedtime is 9:00. "I keep to this routine every day without variation," he told *The Paris Review*. "The repetition itself becomes the most important thing. It's a form of mesmerism. I mesmerize myself to reach a deeper state of mind."

You have joined us here in the pages of this book because you want to write, you want to write more, maybe you want to write something in particular, and you've had the feeling that to do that, you *need* something more. Rituals are a reliable way to make that *more*, to give nourishment in physical form to our longing, and remind us reliably that what we're thinking, feeling, and writing is essential.

Let's make some clear distinctions. Ritual, habit, and practice are not quite the same. Habits get us to the office on time and get our teeth flossed and brushed. *Habits* march along worn grooves in our psyches, or more accurately, along well-traveled neural pathways. Habits are often largely unconscious. *Rituals*, often thought of as solemn and sacred, differ from habits not necessarily in their motions but in their attention and their intention: Ritual is habit and practice made conscious, present, and alive. And *practice*, as we'll use the term here and in the following chapters, refers to a regular pattern of activity we engage in to improve our skill.

Getting ready to write is not actually writing. But getting ready is the place of ritual, and that place is crucial. The step from daily life to writing life can feel like a leap across a chasm. Amid the maze of distractions in our lives, it's easy to 'forget' to turn toward the blank page. Sometimes we actively do not want to walk into the creative fires. Sometimes we need intentional habits which carry us forward across the chasm and bring us back home again on the other side.

I had written in journals and the occasional break-up poem since I was a tween. I carried a knot in my gut of a painful family story for even longer, at first declaring that I would never write a memoir and then acknowledging that the pain and the confusion sown by that seminal experience just wasn't going to go away by itself. I wanted to understand it and had an instinct that writing it down, all of it, might offer me the path to the clarity and relief I sought. I joined a monthly writing group with Joan Hunter called *Beginning a Writing Project,* which became in its regularity and intentionality my first writing practice. Whenever I could, I wrote. When the kids were with their father, when I had at least a few hours or preferably a few days to myself. I did write that story. I edited it and rewrote it at least five times over the almost ten years it took to complete. For two years, I worked with a development editor. It was terrific and arduous. Through it all, I did get a radically new perspective, as well as a sense of ease and new freedom from the story I'd been carrying for so long. It was ten years well spent.

What I didn't get from that first writing experience was a ritual of my own making.

When the ideas for my second book began to simmer, I found my way to another workshop, a *Deep Writing* workshop with Eric Maisel, whose practical expertise focused participants on *getting it done*. I returned from the seminar, declared that I would get up every morning, make my tea, and write for 45 minutes. Every. Morning. And I did. Not quite at the Stephen King level, but almost. I completed the first draft of that book in less than a year and made its final draft ready for agents and publication within two years. It turns out that the math actually works: A page a day equals 365 pages in one year. That's a book, even once you carve away all the excess pages to reveal its essential center.

What I had unknowingly done with that book was to establish a "trigger" to signal the start of the writing day. A ritual. My trigger was English Breakfast tea in the flowered cup. As the water heated and as I set cup and creamer on my little tray, I was already entering the silence, already turning toward the page. Your trigger might be a hot shower or an extra-hot soy latte. Make for yourself a trigger that will reliably remind you that it's writing time when this occurs, and keep it simple.

Julia Cameron, who became known in artist circles for her book *The Artist's Way*, prescribed for her readers two rituals that have since become classic: Morning Pages and the Artist's Date. Her prescription for Morning Pages, which she calls the "bedrock tool of creative recovery," asks us to write every morning before anything else, to write whatever needs to be noticed or whatever needs to be cast aside before the writing day begins. The stuff of dreams and grocery lists and complaints and gratitudes and creativity, these Morning Pages involve writing three long-hand pages without stopping. That's it. You may think of them as similar to the doodles artists make as warmups for a painting project. Now and then, you'll write something you'll want to mine for your work. At the same time, it can be tremendously freeing to write knowing it's pure dross you're writing, and that no one will see it. Think of this as ritual: Morning Pages as intentional *approach* to your practice of writing.

Dulcie began writing in a focused way at age 56 during her mother's grave illness and her primary relationship's death, when she needed to sort through her internal files of feelings and losses. She began with Morning Pages, which became mourning pages as she found herself going back, back, back, through all the deaths, all the losses, and all the ungrieved grief of the previous decades.

She talks of this time now as a gift, though it did not seem so at the time. Day after day, page after page of sorrow and sadness punctuated with tears and snot rolled on and on, always another loss right behind the last one. She kept going for months until there was no headstone left unturned, and when she finished, she printed them out and slid them into a folder called Some of Me. That early ritual of Morning Pages became a folder which became a source of material for her application packet to MFA graduate school the next year and then for her first novel, *Crooked Love*.

> Sometimes I very much doubt whether in the future anyone will be interested in all my tosh. The 'unbosomings of an ugly duckling' will be the title of all this nonsense."
>
> — Anne Frank

Our writing methods can themselves become ritual. Many writers suggest writing long-hand to avoid the distracting process of editing each sentence several times before the next can form. Your trigger to write could be that particular pen, that clipboard, a tidy stack of fresh paper. On the other hand, if you're a highly-charged writer whose words fly out like bats from a cave at dusk, the computer may be the only device that will keep up with your thoughts. This method may work for you, and there's absolutely no harm in trying. But do consider here the ways in which approaching the writing with ritual may help you avoid the computer's endless distracting possibilities. Could you go offline to write, making that moment of clicking the button a statement of intention?

Whichever way best suits you, there will be pauses in your process. When they occur, please do not edit what you've just written. Writing and editing do not live well together. Instead, develop intentional habits for those moments of pause. You might choose a word or a phrase from what you've just written and ask: What is my story of...? Write that. Write as many times as needed, *I don't know what to say*. There's something there. It just may not move in the way you think it should. Writing is not thinking so much as it is following, and sometimes things are just not ready to be said. Some writers say there's no such thing as writer's block, that there simply are times when the words aren't quite ready. We agree.

Beyond the writing triggers and the writing method, you may get interested in creating other rituals.

Before Eline writes, she tends to her plants. She walks around her room to see which leaves need dusting, where the soil has dried out, what new leaves are unfurling. You could say it's a form of procrastinating, finding reasons to not yet sit down with the story. In some ways, that's true. But her walk around her indoor garden has another function too. Some plants take up to two weeks just to unfurl one of their leaves. And if she touches those leaves while they're still in the process of becoming fully formed things, they break or get brown spots. She applies these tiny leaf lessons to her writing: Don't try to pry open with your fingers what's still in the process of becoming a fully formed thing. Give it time, but keep coming back to it. Make sure the soil doesn't dry out. Dust the parts of the story you're hesitant to come back to, they're still shiny underneath. Like your plants, your story might lose some of its leaves in winter. Try to trust the cyclical nature of everything you're surrounded by. With time a new summer of growth will come.

The importance of ritual does not lie in the *discipline* of the act so much as in *intention* and *devotion*. When you move from habit to habit-with-intention, you are already a creator. Writing is its manifestation. Dreams come true.

Let's take a moment to sit with the truth of this statement: When you move from habit to habit-with-intention, you are already a creator. So...

> **What do you most want to create? What is the project you're working on or intending to make? Write this down. "I am writing....". Write it as though it is already in process. Write as though you know what it's about and above all, why it matters, even if you don't yet believe you know these things.**

When we take the time and spend the money to take ourselves on retreat in the Tuscan hills or by the rocky coast of Maine with an intention of coming closer to the Writer in us, the journey of departing from the known world and arriving in a new one becomes a ritual of its own, a hero(ine)'s journey. Without that passage, in our lives at home, it is equally important to consider the boundary between regular time and writing time, or between public space and writing space, and to make the writing time and space a container for all it will need to hold.

As a married mother of two sons, Pam struggled for years to find her reliable writing life, until she realized that she literally needed a room of her own. Now she writes in the new she-shack in the backyard, where she's posted group photos of every Wide Open Writing retreat, most of which she's either attended or tended. We love imagining that she's tuning in to her writing tribe and the writer within every time she sits in that chair.

Our friend Alyson writes in the closet in her bedroom, where she sits on a meditation cushion in front of a small coffee table. When that door is closed, the family is uninvited.

Could you create a space of your own?
Could you find a time, even in the middle of your life?

Could you write on the train to work, in a quiet space on your lunch hour? Could you wake before the house stirs?

Robin is a full-time writer. For the first hour of the morning, she writes in her notebook. She gets the whining out, the bad sentences down, the wayward thoughts and self-absorbed musings out of the way. Next, she reads poetry for its loaded beauty, its magical wonder. Then her imagination runs down and around the pathways toward her work-in-progress or the blank page.

Mary Beth, another mother of two growing children, finds that no matter how hard she's tried, writing does not happen for her either at home or at the office. Periodically she rents a motel room, where she does almost nothing else; as if all the thoughts from all those days when she wasn't able to bring herself to the page held their breath until she could exhale in the quiet and the privacy of her own space.

As some of us know from our religious experiences in childhood, rituals can be elaborate beyond imagination! We are so beautifully designed for developing and practicing ritual that as every succeeding generation adds their symbolic signature to existing rituals, the results can be cumbersome at best. Thanksgiving traditions have a way of gathering momentum in the same way: We eat dinner at 3:00 or at 7:00, Aunt Joan brings the sweet potato casserole with marshmallows, we do or don't eat turkey, it has to be Mom's cranberry sauce or it's not Thanksgiving, we go around the table giving voice to gratitude, we play Christmas carols for the first time this year, we watch football and fall asleep, we play Dictionary or Charades.

In some of our brains, the neural pathways of habit have a tendency to rigidify into compulsions. I know a writer whose habits of desk organizing — pencil sharpening, paper straightening, surface clearing — slowly overtook his writing and his life as though they had amoeba-like lives of their own. His house was remarkable for its cleanliness, but his writing suffered. At some point, in place of a daily writing practice, he developed daily headaches.

But rituals can also be as simple as opening a notebook and closing a notebook, with intention.

Taking four breaths, inhale and exhale to the count of four. Join thumb and index finger to secure a connection with your internal energy. Look at the picture in front of you in your writing space, of Toni Morrison, of the Buddha, of your grandmother, and say Hello. Or Help, or Thanks, or Wow! (*Help, Thanks, Wow.* is the title of a book by Annie Lamott, which in shorthand represents her recommended essential prayers). Say with devotion and intention: I am here to write. I am here to write what is true. I am here to write a story, a poem, a love letter. I am here, asking for help.

Let's write.

From here on, when we offer a prompt for a piece of writing, we'd like you to assume the broadest possible invitation in that prompt. If the prompt asks for a story from your life, consider this potentially as a request for a fictional story or a poem or an essay, and consider engaging as much curiosity as you can. The story you write may be from your life, from the life of someone you know, from a character you're exploring, or from one you don't know you're writing. Consider prompts as inspiration rather than requirement.

> **Bringing in as much information from your senses as you can, tell the story of a ritual that has made a difference in your life. Write for 25 minutes.**

Close your notebook or laptop or phone, take a deep breath and exhale fully. Stand up, making this closure a ritual. Walk around. Go to the bathroom.

Now do or say one more thing that will represent closure of today's writing exercise for you, one thing that you'd like to turn into an intentional habit connected to your writing life. Bow to your page. Bring your hands to your heart. Sigh. Say thank you. It's up to you. This may feel natural and wonderful to do. It may feel awkward and silly. Either way, we invite you to trust the request and your invented "habit" and do it anyway. The ritual you've just created — like salt, like water, like air — is an essential ingredient for growth.

Please read your writing out loud. As we did with the initial write in our opening session, make a note of the words or phrases you loved, were moved by, felt a "charge" in as you read. It's also okay to notice what words or phrases didn't feel quite right; those can become questions to reflect or write on at another moment. From the paragraphs above, I might ask, "What is my story of 'awkward and silly'?"

With this and any future writing practices in this book, when time and interest allow, **you may want to dive in again for another 25 minutes, following a thought that caught your attention in the first write, or a question that sprang to your mind as you read aloud, or a new character you're interested in hearing from.**

Back in Tuscany, this first writing circle closes. The participants, having newly written and read and relaxed, and feeling more connected with one another, wander down the hill to dinner in the open-air dining room where food and wine and conversation flow out into the warm night.

Self-Care and Ritual

What will be your way of soothing and smoothing your writing self after a writing session or a writing day?

Sometimes the writing will be its own reward. Sometimes you want to create an even stronger connection between writing and feeling really, really good. Consider, especially as you're developing intentional habits that will serve you for your *entire writing life*, the power of joining the writing to a counter-balancing practice of something that soothes you. Yoga. A warm bath. The gentlest tea in your most beautiful cup. Massage. Going outdoors. Meditation. Sex. Laughter.

For me, yoga has become the go-to place for my weary or overcharged mental energy to smooth out. For others, that go-to place may be Starbucks. Or the backyard hot tub. Or a phone call with a friend. Whatever it is, add intention and devotion to habit. Make it ritual. Call it that. Claim it.

Nikki regularly hikes in a nearby state park, clearing her mind amid tall shushing pines and groves of old oaks. In Tuscany, she has a favorite tree she likes to write underneath. Its branches provide shade from the hot Italian afternoon, and an acorn or two sometimes falls on her notebook. One year, when she couldn't come to the Italy retreat, she took a walk in her favorite woods. As if the oaks received a message from her favorite tree, acorns dropped from above.

Dulcie received a call from a friend in Vermont: "Hey, Dulc, come take this TM class with me."

"TM?" Dulcie said.

"Transcendental Meditation, you'll love it, and I think it'll help you calm down and focus. That's what it's doing for me."

Calming down and focusing were both yearnings that Dulcie reached towards but hadn't yet found to be reliably achievable. So, she went to Vermont and took the class. And now, TM is a regular part of her day. She wouldn't miss it - twice a day, first at the beginning of the day and then at the end of the workday. It is not clear how much of the gain she experiences comes from the meditation itself and how much from taking twenty minutes and allowing herself to slide down under the noise, trusting that she will return intact. She has come to believe that the time spent away is worth at least as much as what she does with the time, the gains as much about the ritual as its contents. And perhaps that is always the way of ritual.

Sometimes my yoga practice is a daily one. Sometimes I loosen the grip and come to the mat with less regularity – but when this happens, I'm likely to lose ground quickly. My bones and joints act cranky. So, I try to practice regularly, sometimes with bliss and sometimes without inspiration but with the necessary discipline and devotion to get myself to the mat. That's the hardest part. Once every year or so, I go somewhere where someone else will guide me in day after day of yoga immersion, morning and evening, with a yoga dance break in the middle and something to contemplate in between. In that immersive time, my daily practice opens out into its full expression. It also serves to fuel my home practice for months to come.

What ritual will you choose to close your writing practice for the day?

5
Practice

"I talked incessantly about being a writer and read books about writing and imagined, in great detail, my life as a writer. I did everything except write...Finally I sat down and thought very seriously about exactly what it took to be a writer. I came to the conclusion that one thing, absolutely, was required: writing."

— Katy DiCamillo

Writers must write. That's all there is to it.

The intention to write and the rituals of writing serve to bring our minds and hearts to the page, where the *practice* begins..

Who hasn't heard the maxim, "Write every day"? But who writes every day? What if you're not inspired, or you're overly busy or tired or frantic or sad or too happy, or the sun is shining? And what's so special about everyday-ness? Stephen King, in his classic book *On Writing,* tells us that he'd like to say that he doesn't actually write *every single day.* But in fact, he goes on to say, he does. Write. Every. Single. Day. Even Christmas.

One definition of the word *practice* in the Oxford Dictionary is "the actual application (italics mine) of a method, idea or belief." Principles matter. Theory matters. Research can be infinitely fascinating. But "actual application" is, finally, the only way to get better at tennis or cooking or writing.

And daily practice is the most trustworthy exercise.

In the course of writing this book, the usual interruptions and distractions marched in and out of my days, wearing their clothing of urgency and temptation. Sometimes I left the desk and followed them. When I did, when more than 24 hours passed between writing sessions, it was as if a magic portal had begun to close. Re-entry through the doorway became more difficult. At first I would have to go over all the preceding chapters to remember where I was and what I thought should happen next. If a few days had gone by, I noticed that I had forgotten not only where I was, but why I would bother. The more time passed, the more I lost track of anything at all about my writer self. And I'm not alone in this: Have you had the experience of feeling as though you have lost all connection to the creative writer in you, that it is on an island in the far distance, that you have nothing to say anyway?

As you are in continual relation — or as the poet David Whyte puts it, in *conversation* — with your work, your family, your friends, you are also in relation to your Writer. And what is the nature of that relationship? Is it casual or distant? Is it laden with difficulties? Is it intimate, respectful, and honest? Would you like to make it better? It is our promise to you that you can do that.

Write every day. That could be the declaration you make to yourself as you make your way through the pages of this retreat-in-writing. If this is your intention, follow through on the declaration. In time, you will find that the door stands open. You will have the experience of witnessing other wonderful things gathering around your intentional habit as if it has magnetic force. You may find thoughts flowing more easily, the dilemma of the previous day having untangled itself while you sleep, the shopping list you write one day making way for an explosion of clarity the next.

Because I have been doing it for quite a while now, and because my children are grown, and because I live with another writer, I write just about anywhere and everywhere in my home. Some days, like a cat, I follow the sun. Some days, I stay close to the woodstove. The essential ingredients of my practice are the invisible but sacred containers I make of uninterrupted space and time. Writing long-hand means I'm doing Morning Pages or proprioceptive writing[2], the two ways I spill out whatever is ready to pour onto the page. Coming to the computer means I'm prepared to write in the current project.

For the better part of 20 years, through all manner of family machinations and work changes, Dulcie has written to a writing pen pal nearly every day. Her morning ritual, her practice.

Malcolm Gladwell, in his book *Outliers*, popularized the notion that 10,000 hours of focused, deliberate practice are required for mastery. The original declaration came from the discovery that the most skilled of student violinists had amassed that many hours of practice before they were 20 years old. Since then, refinements have been added to the evocative 10,000 hour generalization. Is practice important, even crucial? Yes. But motivation for practice and the emotions connected with practicing are also crucial to the ultimate value of that practice.

Practice without heart will not go far. What are the deeper motivations, the aspirations, the connections with purpose and long-term values, that make your writing practice relevant to you? We'll look into these questions in chapters to come.

Sometimes emotions have been considered the bull in the china shop of our psyches, as though they get in the way of serious effort and break the china of our best intentions with their

---

[2] Proprioceptive writing, made popular by Linda Trichter Metcalf in *Writing The Mind Alive*, focuses on exploring the contents of one's own mind with timed, unedited, practices of writing whatever emerges.

waywardness. But psychologists have been discovering that instead of suppressing emotions in order to get the job done, embracing them and listening to them is actually a path to greater effectiveness and greater emotional intelligence. This is good news for writers: If we go where our emotions go and let them guide us to the heart of what we want to write, we in turn allow them to further our practice.

Let's imagine that you haven't yet accumulated 10,000 hours of deliberate, focused, motivated, emotionally relevant practice as a writer. Could you begin now? Not by counting the hours, although that's an interesting distraction in itself, but by committing to a practice? Could you commit to writing every day, for 25 minutes? For 10 minutes?

A very simple practice helper for you might be the Pomodoro method[3], developed by Francesco Cirillo in the 1980s, which essentially breaks up project work into manageable bundles, usually 25 minutes in length, followed by short breaks. Other authors have found that 90-minute work segments reflect their natural concentration cycles. Experiment with the element of time. What is enjoyable, effective, and sustainable for you?

Perhaps your circumstances are such that you're really not going to write every single day. Are there other options? Mary Beth, the writer who escaped to motels, has written many published essays that way. Jack wrote an entire memoir over the period of a month in a rented cabin. You will be most successful if you find a pace and a ritual that works for you and let it do its work.

Writing is a practice, and it is through the regular practice of ordinary acts that the world is changed.

---

3 Cirillo, Francesco. https://francescocirillo.com/products/the-pomodoro-technique-book-us-edition. The beauty of this technique lies in its simplicity. Numerous online sources describe in greater detail the steps to Pomodoro practice.

When the world paused for the COVID-19 pandemic, we soon didn't know whether we were experiencing the beginning or the middle or coming to the end of that strange hiatus. There was so much we didn't know. But the gift of that time – the way the world irrevocably changed, our physical bodies going nowhere – lay in the possibility we were given to reawaken ongoing practices. In daily devotion to the mat or the page, real growth happened, along the blundering path of believing in the process and ourselves even when there seemed to be no concrete reason to do so.

That's how we're writing this book. Daily. With a practice of trust, even when we don't know where it's going. With devotion born of knowing that our inspiration to write this book matters, we engage curiosity and wonder, remarkable preventive medicines for self-doubt and writer's block. We write on. And that's what we're encouraging you to do. As best you can, write on.

6
Inspiration

"The universe buries strange jewels within us all, and then stands back (to watch us) find them."

— Elizabeth Gilbert

Tuscany. Midday heat shimmers over the vineyards and hills. A colorful thread of riders weaves across the far ridges as the farm's Icelandic horses travel the long views and the dusty pathways of the ancient Camino di San Francisco. Wherever we turn, inspiration lives here; in the stones and the patterns of the hillsides, in weathered historic plaques marking Etruscan, Roman, World War I stories. In the ancient quiet, in the surprise of a ripe fig at eye level on its branch.

Spirit. Inspiration. Aspiration. Let's explore these words as they relate to an energized writing life.

Spirit most conservatively defined means breath or wind. But it also means more than that, in that it has been taken to mean the power behind the breath, a power whose origins are mysterious. Here we'll use the word *spirit* to mean that which animates and empowers, that inner force which makes us truly and fully alive. The wind beneath our wings.

Inspiration and aspiration can be seen as vectors in a life imbued with spirit. If spirit enlivens us, inspiration refers to what specifically motivates us, what lights up that inner spirited flame. Inspiration strikes when we have a new vision, a bright idea, a flash of insight. Inspiration rises from the light and shadow of the green and grey and gold Tuscan hills, from an ache in the belly, from a moment of contemplation, from a song heard on the breeze. And inspiration can rise from aspiration.

Aspiration is felt as the strong desire for something great, the dream toward a horizon we cannot yet see. We humans are unique in the natural world, not primarily because of our opposable thumbs or our consciousness. We are not the only soulful beings on Earth. However, we are apparently unique in our capacity to aspire. Wide Open Writing rose out of aspiration: We wanted to travel and write and do that with other people who wanted to travel and write. And we were fueled by deeper aspirations as well: To generate healing in the world through the power of creativity and community. To that end, we were right in believing this would be well-received.

What we underestimated was the effect that immersion in collective creative vigor would have on our creative output – both in quantity and in quality. One of the most rewarding benefits of being part of Wide Open Writing has been watching and being part of each other's growth. Growing together. You too have come to the pages of this book because of your aspiration, and now you are a part of a collaborative creative venture.

Everything in existence began somewhere in consciousness first. And every new step begins with a blend of aspiration and inspiration.

We begin this section of the retreat with closer attention to the very particular aspiration that brings you here. "Don't ask," said the noted African-American theologian and civil rights activist Howard Thurman, "what the world needs. *Ask what makes you come alive, and go do it.* Because what the world needs is people who have come alive." The clearer our connections to our essential aspirations, the more powerfully our creative channels will hum and vibrate and radiate with inspiration, and thus with greatness.

Before you go any further, let's explore. If you have a timer, this will be an excellent place to use it to create a container for several short pieces of writing. We'll present prompts for four short writing exercises, with the suggestion that you pause as you complete each one. Breathe consciously, stand up and stretch, or sit quietly with the feeling of what you've just written.

> **For the first exercise, please take five minutes to write about the reason behind your decision to take this "retreat," the Why.**

It's to get my writing juices flowing. It's to tell the story of my ancestors who fled the pogroms. I want to have something to pass on to my children and grandchildren. I need to discharge the story that's stuck in my gut so someone, and maybe that someone is me, can understand what happened.

Write what should not be forgotten."

— Isabel Allende

Please pause now.

And then, we'll take it deeper. What inspires you? Jewish tradition holds a space for the concept of Tikkun, the intergenerational paradox we are born with and born to heal. Psychologist James Hillman speaks of the "soul's code." Stephen Cope, psychologist and yoga scholar, calls us to the "great work of (our) life." These are all ways of speaking about both aspiration and inspiration, the driving forces behind all of who we are. And that's what we're getting at.

For the second exercise, take five minutes to list without stopping or editing, repeatedly completing the sentence, "I love…."

Please pause to feel these words.

Now, take five minutes to list, "As a child I loved…"

And one more exploration: Take five minutes to write your most profound dreams, your "Why am I here?" reflections. Even if you don't know what these dreams are, write anyway.

This is not the time to consider the "reality" of those dreams or loves, or to contend with obstacles that might arise, practicalities of time, money, or proper certification. First things first. Write and keep writing, gathering up whatever may be wanting to whisper its longings to you. Reflecting on words like obsession, desire, or prayer may also help.

Now take a break, get a drink of water, and give yourself a few minutes to integrate what you've just written.

What has always been there, what lingers at the edges of your awareness? Take some time with these lists, noticing what strikes you. What themes arise, what shows up more than once, what do you see there that draws you in? Be gentle with yourself. Everything that exists begins in consciousness. Writing thoughts on paper brings your ideas, visions, and dreams from the mind to the real world, and this tiny miraculous fact is one of the secrets of manifestation. If you know where you're going, you're more likely to get there. If you don't know where you're going, you'll probably wind up somewhere else. If you don't know what you most aspire to, likely it won't come your way. But even turning our thoughts in the direction of what we *might* most want invites new cellular connections, new growth, and expansion.

"So long as you write what you wish to write, that is all that matters; and whether it matters for ages or only for hours, nobody can say."

— Virginia Woolf

At the end of our very first Tuscany retreat, before we even knew that we were Wide Open Writing, we held a salon-style reading together in the warm September afternoon under a spreading chestnut tree. I read the last pages of my just-completed novel to the group, a story that ended with what I called a storm of Biblical proportions. Rain and hail and wind and even frogs fell from the sky, and the people of the story took to their houses and their churches and their prayers, even if they hadn't previously been known to pray. The next morning, our Tuscany retreat ended. We rode back together to Florence, and some of us went to Florence's remarkable Central Market to buy dried porcini mushrooms and parmesan and pasta, to eat pizza and gelato, to soak up the vibe of our last days in Italy. In the middle of our lunch, the enormous basket-like lighting fixtures in the high ceiling of the Market began to sway a bit wildly, and a sound like a low-flying plane cut through the clatter and hum of the busy marketplace. We noticed that although we were indoors, we were feeling a lot of wind from somewhere. And then it began to pour. Indoors. Vendors scrambled. Tourists and business people huddled close to the walls of the market building. One brave couple stayed at their table under umbrellas in the middle of this vast space, while most of us stared in awe at the scene of the swaying light fixtures and the slanting indoor rain.

After about 30 minutes, the commotion stopped as suddenly as it had begun. We clambered out of our hiding places, trooped down long staircases streaming with rain, and stepped outside. What had only moments before been a vibrant outdoor leather market under tents surrounding the Central building stood decimated, tent coverings shredded, vendors scrambling. And the ground was covered with white stuff that looked to this native New Englander like rock salt. It was hail, three or four inches deep.

Maybe hailstorms happen all the time in Florence in September. This one closed the Uffizi gallery. This storm made news across the Atlantic in the Washington Post. We came to believe this storm had something to do with the reading we'd held the day before. Writing our thoughts on paper brings them from the world of the mind to the physical reality.

Nikki worked full-time at a newspaper in California while pursuing her MFA through Goddard College. In 2008, recession hit the industry hard. For a while, she tried to juggle long hours at work while working on her creative thesis, a post-apocalyptic story centered on a protagonist named Sandra McCarthy. Eventually, though, her work-school schedule reached a breaking point, and she faced a choice between continuing her education or keeping her job. When her parents suggested she move home to the Midwest and keep going with her graduate program, she hesitated but ultimately chose to nurture her creativity. After packing her things into storage, driving home, and moving back into the bedroom she'd had at age seventeen, she still wasn't sure about this big choice. One day, in this state of questioning the entire idea, she found herself lost in a new neighborhood in the growing town. She stopped the car to get her bearings, checked the street names where she'd paused, and saw she was at the corner of Sandra and McCarthy. Not only was it the right move, but returning to surroundings familiar to Nikki as a young adult changed the course of her thesis – she changed her protagonist from an adult to a teenager, and the story flowed much more easily as a stronger manuscript. Plus, her old position at the newspaper was eliminated six months after her departure.

She paid attention to her longings. She followed her aspirations, not without question, but with devotion. And the world offered back its own kind of support. Take this to heart. Act as though it's true. Act as though it matters that you write what you're writing.

> Wherever you go, you meet part of your story."
>
> — Eudora Welty

It matters what we write. We don't begin to know the mechanics of the whole process. We don't really know whether the Italian hailstorm was a coincidence, or an idea I created and put out in the real world for its manifestation, or a vision given to me from the future, already existing somewhere in consciousness. Maybe it doesn't matter. Perhaps what matters is to remember that when we write, when we create, we're joining forces with the creative powers of the entire universe. We're allowed to write whatever comes to our minds. We have to; it's all we have. The particular channel that is your creative path in the world has its own setting – country western, hip hop, jazz, comedy, opera, gospel, rap – and that's what you'll play.

There is something each of us is here to do. James Hillman, psychologist, suggests that the acorn, the kernel of our nature, is inborn far more than it is grafted onto us by experience. He tells the story of Mozart, who had strong tutors guiding him from the start, but also of the famous Spanish bull-fighter who not only had no connection to the world of bullfighting as a child but who hid behind his mother's skirts as the bulls ran through the streets. Hillman proposes that this innate acorn within us wants expression, and that it will seek that expression whether or not its circumstances are encouraging.

> **Look at the lists you've created thus far. Look at your loves and your dreams. Begin to create a statement of the oak or maple or apple tree that is you.**
> *I am here to act as a channel for divine beauty in the world through artistic expression.*
> *I am a builder of worlds, a dreamer of what could be better.*
> *I am a seeker and speaker of truth.*

Make your statement. Say it aloud. Stand up and repeat it. Tell this deepest life dream to one or two people you're willing to trust with something this precious. Make a picture or a sign or create a totem to set near your writing space.

This is what you're doing here, and this is what we're doing here. This is the wind beneath the wings of your creative spirit. Without that wind, the doldrums. Against the wind, we struggle to make headway, the passage harsh. With the wind, we soar.

There is no greater agony than bearing an untold story inside you."
— Maya Angelou

7
Silence

"And don't we all, with fierce hunger, crave a cave of solitude, a space of deep listening — full of quiet darkness and stars, until finally we hear a syllable of God, echoing in the cave of our hearts?"

— Macrina Wiederkehr

When we offered our first writing retreat in Tuscany, it occurred to us that we could spend early mornings in a kind of sacred silence. Even the three retreat leaders didn't meet this idea with universal acclaim. Maybe extroverts were more likely to bristle at the thought of enforced quiet. Maybe people who'd come to love the practices of yoga and meditation were more likely to long for spacious space, for timeless time, those potential by-products of silence. For ten years, I had staffed weekend workshops during which we held silence for the entire weekend with the exception of the group exercises. I liked it. I loved the discovery that in silence, people could genuinely stay with ourselves. I loved not having to spend energy asking one another awkward questions: *So. Where are you from?* when what we most needed to do was stay present to the flow or flood of internal stories that had brought us all to the workshop in the first place.

WOW tried it. Some of our favorite images of that first workshop are of individual women sitting alone in the slanted morning light: Drinking coffee on a stone wall at the edge of truffle forests. Writing in a journal at the dining table under the pergola, green-eyed cat at her side, the sun sliding down her back. Sitting cross-legged on the yoga patio, eyes closed, dropping in. And we love at least as much the memories of greeting one another from that silence with our smiles, our eyes, with gestures exaggerated by the attempts not to speak, with quiet chuckles.

"Talk is a way to warm up for the big game – the hours you write alone with your pen and notebook."

— Natalie Goldberg

    To the surprise of many of us, we loved this practice. Rather than being more awkward and more isolating than meeting one another with words, we found that we felt delightfully connected in the silence. Dulcie walks by Pam and lays a hand on her shoulder. Pam's head leans to rest on Dulcie's hand. Touch becomes another kind of connection, more profound than words. We meet, as we have and as we will throughout the retreat, in a place of spacious silence, a space from which when it's time, the words will arise. As Louis Armstrong said, with all our stories, with all our gestures, we're really saying *I love you*.

    Paradox abounds in a writer's life. While we fully honor the importance of ritual, much of creativity also manifests in the willingness, the need even, to break out of ruts. As humans, we naturally create structures that become traditions, and then habits, and then, sometimes, mindlessness. Rituals go awry when they become mindless. Sometimes, we need to break habits, if only to engage new curiosity about life without those habits.

Silence instead of chatter. Gather yourself before you spend yourself. Listen to the morning.

Julia Cameron is a firm believer in the power of silence. "For an artist," she says, "withdrawal is essential. Until we experience the freedom of solitude, we cannot connect authentically." Retreat in order to re-connect.

The morning silence became a touchstone of our WOW retreats, just as the retreats themselves became touchstones for writers who needed room and permission to seek fertile quiet within while being held in creative community.

Suppose you can't travel to Italy or Mexico or Maine to join us for the full retreat experience. Suppose we couldn't hold retreats for a time as the world recovered from the shock and devastation of a global pandemic. In that case, we could at least seek a spacious quiet where we were.

Try it.

Spend a day (an hour, a morning) in intentional silence.

Go for a walk, longer than 30 minutes. Listen to the outside world. Listen to your inside world. Notice from your silence what happens when you encounter other humans. Notice the crowded freeway of your mind. Notice the restlessness, the desire to turn on the news or listen to music. Listen to nature, the quiet, the stillness, instead. How much of what you've heard could you capture on paper? Notice any peace that may arise.

Surround your writing with silence.

Don't talk before you write. And don't speak until you've closed the door on the writing practice for the day. Let the people in your home environment know you need to create what a writer friend calls "a reverie of your own design." When you come to your writing space, take four deep breaths before you do anything else. If you don't have room in your life for these moments, create them. You are a creator, remember?

Texts and emails are talking.

Write for 25 minutes from the silence, on the feel of this time for you, letting your thoughts spread wide enough to contemplate the place of silence in your life. Notice aloud the quality of your relationship to silence. Pose questions about any of your characters and how they might relate to a time of silence in their lives.

8
Vision

"Know that the Creator lives and moves and breathes within you. So those dreams? Risk them. Those words? Write them. Those hopes? Believe them."
—Elora Nicole Ramirez

You picked up this book, and you've gotten this far. Your dreams live on.

We are made to create. And yet...how much we've tried to suppress that vital force! We are both dreamers and the ones who seek to destroy our own dreams. There is nothing unusual about attempting to dim our light, just as there is nothing inevitable about that dimming. Our dreams will not stay buried.

As our writing group meets again in the soft light of the Tuscan morning, we've established some practices around how we'll come to our writing; we've written about our dreams and inspirations, we've made space for silence. Now, we're ready to make dreams come true.

WOW likes to create powerful themes for our retreats, with titles like Writing the Wild, Writing the Elements, Thresholds, Grief, and Rebirth. As you may already have guessed, we're calling the retreat contained in these pages *Manifesting Your Dreams*. As you move through succeeding chapters, you'll notice that we're getting more and more specific about how exactly manifestation can happen through and for our writing. At the same time, we're developing skills in working with the inevitable obstacles that sneak into our creative spaces. And we do all of this by writing, so it's dual-purpose.

We use generative writing to open creative channels within us as we simultaneously cultivate the strategies we'll need to keep those channels clear.

In the preceding chapters, we've uncovered some fundamental dreams, dreams we might call *life purpose* dreams.

Let's turn one of those dreams into a *goal*. The magic carpet you're sailing has a rudder and a tiller, and you are steering. Suppose a *life purpose* you've claimed is that you are a channel for divine beauty in the world. In that case, you might begin to imagine a particular realm of your life – your writing, your relationships, your health, your finances – and to think about how you will express your life purpose in that channel. The place we are looking draws us forward toward our goal.

Choose a dream.

Imagine this dream in its complete form. Imagine it has already come true in living color, in its textures and smells and sounds, in all its specifics. Imagine the book on the bookshelf on display. Imagine yourself on the book tour, the podcast, the Broadway show. Now please **write down this imagined goal with as much elaboration as you can muster, using the present tense.** Remember, writing thoughts on paper brings ideas to the physical realm. "I am walking down Fifth Avenue in New York, past a Barnes and Noble bookstore. It's autumn, the street is bustling, and there's an exciting chill in the air. I pause at the window of the store, where my book *From Our Birth*, its beautiful font and cover collage of green trees and dark eyes and flowing water catching the eye, has pride of place in the display of current bestsellers and staff favorites. A woman pauses next to me. We smile at each other. "Have you read that book?" she asks. "We're going to read it for book club. I've heard it's wonderful!"

The more you fill in the dream, the more you condense energy into form, thus creating its reality. The wind beneath your wings lifts the carpet, you set your sights on the far shore, and you aim for that white lighthouse with the red roof standing high over the rocky coast. Winds shift, currents cross and swirl, you become mesmerized by the beauty of sky and sea, and still you aim for the lighthouse. That's the difference between a dream and a goal. Goals contain the vector of getting where you want to go.

When Carolyn Chute, the author of the *Beans of Egypt, Maine*, wanted to meet a man she could spend her life with, she decided to dream him into existence. She used clippings from magazines to invent a man with a plaid shirt and an old green truck, a man she subsequently met and married and lives with to this day — over forty years later.

In 2010, Vanessa was working as a singer on a cruise ship. Because she was only performing a couple of nights a week, she found herself with a fair amount of downtime. After finding a treasure trove of old magazines underneath her bed, Vanessa began her 'Vision Boarding' practice. She would turn on some music, spread herself out on the cabin floor, and flip through the magazines, cutting out images and words that resonated with her. Once she'd collected a drawer-full of clippings, she bought a self-adhesive photo album and began the process of laying these images out on the pages. Nearly ten years later, Vanessa rediscovered the photo album and was shocked to find that many of the visions she'd had on that cruise ship had manifested in her life. She didn't know, in 2010, when she cut out that picture of a flight attendant looking chic in her uniform that two years later, she would win a role in the National Tour of "Catch Me If You Can" the musical, and spend 8 shows a week in a 'Pan Am Stewardess' costume. When she cut out a picture of a masseuse, she didn't know that nine years later, she would travel to Thailand and certify to be a Thai massage therapist. And she certainly didn't know that when she covered an image of a martini with a big fat X as if to say 'no more'...that she would, eight years later, choose to stop drinking. In retrospect, Vanessa believes that *some part of her* knew what she was doing on the floor of her officer's cabin in the middle of the Atlantic. Her journey of manifestation was just beginning.

Let's play with this.

Gather materials for your own Vision Board: Corkboard, scissors, tape, pins, glue stick, markers, and stickers if you want to embellish, magazines from which you can cut images and quotes, and photos, sayings, pictures of places, reminders of people, just about anything that inspires you. Give yourself an hour or two of private time, or if circumstances allow and you're in the mood, invite a friend to do this with you. Make a portrait of your dream come true.

Because you are a writer, you could also use this process to understand a character in your writing project. The Vision Board exercise is the "I want..." song that arrives early in the Broadway musical, the dream that gives direction and drive to the entire show. It's the "I Have A Dream" song from *Mamma Mia* and the "I Have A Dream" speech from Martin Luther King Jr.

> *As a way of bringing the Vision Board practice to the page,* **use your visual exercise as a prompt to write a story. Whether you'd like to write about your life or the life of a character in your fiction, how did this vision come to fruition? What's the story behind the story? Write for 30 minutes.**

Notice where your understanding expands and how that may change your feelings about yourself or this character as well.

Vision and Beliefs

> And by the way, everything in life is writable about if you have the outgoing guts to do it, and the imagination to improvise. The worst enemy to creativity is self-doubt."
>
> — Sylvia Plath

You might have noticed that in the goal we envisioned above, the dreamer is walking by an actual brick-and-mortar bookstore. You may have seen that in her dream, people are bustling down a New York City street. At the time of this writing, both of these phenomena have become quite rare. Her goal as she envisions it may not be *realistic*.

External obstacles occur on the way to our happy places. Many of us are prevented from achieving what we most want in our lives by those obstacles. We don't have the money to take the time, we don't have the time, we have limitations and disabilities that mean that even if we had the money or the time, we physically couldn't do what's required. We don't have the degree or the certificate. Etcetera. And many of the obstacles we encounter, many obstacles we perceive to be external reality, arise from filters in our own eyes.

Many years ago, when I was first working as a psychotherapist in a teaching hospital and realizing that hospital work was not for me, I knew I wanted to work from home close to my two young children. I wanted to be in private practice, but I didn't want to work in the evenings or on weekends: I fell asleep regularly before 9:00 pm, whether I intended to or not, and weekends were for family. Therefore, since all psychotherapists keep evening hours to accommodate their clients' work schedules, I knew I couldn't start a private practice.

Does that make sense? Of course, it does. And, of course, it doesn't. What if the belief underlying my perception of the external barriers was in fact an internal obstacle? What if I could change the entire picture without changing anything at all in the outer world? That. Is. Magic. And that is a central tenet of manifestation practices of all kinds.

Somehow an idea came to me. Somehow I decided to become a therapist who didn't work evenings or weekends. I made up and wrote down exactly what my ideal practice would look like, and in very little time at all, this dream came true.

Most often, the obstacles we encounter on the way to our beautiful goals are at least partially internal blocks. This means that we have considerably more power over them than we typically imagine. And most of these obstacles are related to the clouding of our vision by fundamental, often unexamined *beliefs.*

Can you think of a belief about yourself that you may have discovered belatedly was no longer true?

Dulcie's friend Chuck was on the telephone with a prospective employer he planned to meet at a restaurant downtown. He described himself to the employer as blond and chubby. They set a time to meet, and hung up from the call. The man Dulcie was looking at across the table from her was 6 feet tall, brown-haired with glasses, and on the slim side of average weight. He described himself to this person as the boy he looked like at 8 years old! Such an excellent example of an obvious and unexamined belief.

Far more of our beliefs, while equally long-lasting, are not quite so physically obvious. They're buried in the basement of our consciousness. We are handed so many ideas by well-meaning parents, education systems, religious dogma, and by what we see in our peers. And beliefs, once established, tend to remain forever whether or not they're useful or accurate! Is it true that I'm not good enough, that I'm a klutz, that I could never do public speaking, that you aren't smart enough or worthy enough, that any of us is honestly just not creative enough? Is it helpful in some way to hold that belief? For some of us, the idea that we're not good at the business end of the writing world has kept us safe from risking the failure we'd feel if we got rejected. So in that way, it's arguably been helpful. But we could ask if we really want to keep that belief, and we could learn to change any belief we no longer wish to carry. We can learn to substitute far more exciting and helpful beliefs for the crusty old ones.

If I act like those kids, I'll be popular. Nobody likes me. I'll never be normal. It's not a good idea to be smart. I can't trust anyone. No one likes a show-off. I'm too sensitive. God takes care of everything. I don't believe in God. People are out to get you. Being an artist isn't something grownups do. Feed a cold, starve a fever. COVID exists. COVID is a hoax.

You get the idea. Beliefs, many of them established by others and implanted before we had any choice in the matter, shape our personalities and therefore our paths. The difference between success and stagnation in any realm is most often not about talent but about what we believe and what we do with that talent.

Our friend Lion Goodman has come up with a powerful technique for changing those underlying beliefs that plague rather than serve us. Called the Belief Closet[4], this work takes students through an

---

4 http://clearyourbeliefs.com is the home site for Lion Goodman's Belief Closet work.

in-depth process that's fun, easy, creative, and effective; and that we'll sample here. Lion claims that by working with beliefs in this way, we can truly and deeply change our lives at levels impossible to achieve by affirmations or acting as-if. We must, he says, go to the foundations.

Let's try it. This exercise begins with a guided visualization and continues with a writing prompt. The ideal visualization experience offers guidance to you while you simply listen and receive the information that comes. While it's harder to do this on an individual retreat, there are a couple of things you might want to try. For the fullest experience, you could ask someone to read these instructions to you, or you could record yourself reading them. Barring either of those, we recommend reading one paragraph of the visualization, closing your eyes to connect with your internal experience, and then reading on, following that with closing eyes again, and continuing in that manner until the visualization is complete.

First, get in touch with a belief you carry that you might be ready to change.

Let yourself feel how that belief lives in your body; literally where you feel it, and how? Is it accompanied by a headache or a knot in your stomach? Does it feel like lethargy, pressure, excitement?

Imagine yourself in a beautiful private room equipped with a large closet and a large mirror whose reflection only you can see. Take in the details of this room.

Imagine the outfit you're wearing that represents this belief you might be willing to change. How does it fit you? What textures is it made of? What colors? What do you notice about what you look like and how you feel in that outfit? Take it around the room for a walk and see what kind of movement is called forth by the belief and its outfit.

Do you want to change this belief? Do you know what you want to believe now? If your opinion has been that you are invisible, perhaps you'd like believe that you matter. If you have believed that you can't be trusted, maybe you'd like to think of yourself as a reliable person.

Taking your time to imaginarily remove every last scrap of the clothing associated with the old belief, letting yourself see in detail what you're doing to get rid of it (burn? trash? drown?). Make sure you dispose of it completely.

Begin to allow an image of the new belief to form. Go to your imaginary closet and open it to reveal outfits of every possible color and cut and material, from business suits to angel wings to bear suits and rainbow coats. Let your imagination wander through the closet until you find something that speaks to the new belief you're aiming to incorporate.

Put on this outfit and notice the feel, the fit, the look, the way you move.

Before you leave this room, decide whether you'd like to wear the outfit you've chosen into the rest of your life. If this new belief is one that belongs with you at all times, you have the option of invisibilizing it to wear under any other clothing and in any situation. If it's more of a special occasion belief, you can return it to the closet to be there when you need it.

Take a few moments to pause before opening your eyes and returning to the space you're in now.

From here, write a story bringing together the characters and outfits you discovered in the Belief Closet exercise. Let them meet and watch what happens. Write for 25 minutes.

We like thinking of beliefs as outfits, which is close to what is factual about how they come to us — often as hand-me-downs — as well as about our power to change them, more than we might have imagined!

> I believe in belief."
>
> — Dulcie Witman

Visions. Goals. Beliefs. Dreams made visible. Where there was a blank page, words are born. Out of the ethers, from the tap-tap-tapping at the door of the soul and the whispers of aspiration, come stories whose time is now. Believe these stories. You are their scribe.

9
Positivity

"We have been taught to believe that negative equals realistic and positive equals unrealistic."

— Susan Jeffers

Our brains have evolved to scan for problems. If we catch a glimpse of that saber-toothed tiger heading our way, our well-adapted brains have us on the run or brandishing swords before we've even thought about it. Fight, flight or freeze, and thus, survive. It's an excellent strategy, in the short run. Our myelinated neurons – myelin being the super-speed reactivity component of our neural structures, the special sauce that creates reaction before we've even caught up with the action we're reacting to – have kept us safe for centuries. But. When we look at the entire world, at our writing, for instance, through a myelinated lens, we will usually feel like something is wrong.

Our brains don't waste their energy keeping track of what's right. Consider the long-term romantic relationship in which those tiny lovely things that used to mean so much now pale in relation to the unpleasant weight of the unwashed dishes, the dirty socks on the floor, and that habit s/he has of eating pretzels in bed. It's adaptation. We zero in on threats.

Similarly, because threat is at the core of our neurochemical navigation systems, we learn to think critically. At the most fundamental level, our brains operate on binary, no-yes, processes. Threat or Safety. Criticism or Appreciation. Fear or Love. We learn that judging is safer than appreciating. We learn to appreciate negativity for the ways it saves us from physical, social and emotional danger. Our chemical survival strategies of self-protection activate as we naturally avoid what is likely to hurt and approach what we expect to help. But here's the kicker for any creative artist: When self-protection is activated, risks become dangerous and creativity comes to a halt.

"Just as water lilies retract when sunlight fades, so do our minds when positivity fades," is the poetic conclusion drawn by a group of social psychology researchers who compared creative output after seeing images of fear/anger vs. joy/contentment.[5]

In the generative world of WOW's writing retreats, we're interested in getting past self-protection networks in favor of self-actualization, where creativity, joy, and aliveness soar. And we've learned some things about how to do that.

> Learning to take in the good is like fully and mindfully breathing in life: It allows us to access our inner strengths, vitality, creativity and love."
>
> — Tara Brach, *Radical Acceptance*

Yes, our brains are hard-wired for negativity. But we can change that. In the words of Suzanne Kingsbury, founder of a beautiful writing method called Gateless, "When we don't focus on what is wrong, it falls away." Imagine that. Imagine the radical shift this could make in our minds, in our relationships, in our culture, in our educational systems. Imagine what will happen in any of these realms when we focus not on calling out errors but on affirming grace, beauty, and power. Now that we aren't in physical danger, at least during our writing retreats, we can learn to access and expand and eventually live in the higher intelligence of positivity. That is the core of Wide Open Writing's mission. None of us has yet graduated to living in a mind of steady-state positivity. Still, everything we're learning about neuroanatomy and overall wellness reminds us that this positivity is where it's at. And it is undoubtedly where good writing lives.

> Research is beginning to reveal that positive thinking is about much more than being happy or displaying an upbeat attitude. Positive thoughts can actually create real value in your life and help you build skills that last much longer than a smile."
>
> — James Clear, HuffPost

Let's get to writing.

Consider your own experiences (or those of a character you're interested in) of being greeted with positivity or negativity, of praise or criticism. Tell a story about one or more of those experiences. What did you learn about yourself, about life?

Write for 30 minutes, and when you've finished writing, please read on below before you read this writing aloud.

---

[5] Frederickson 2009, *Positivity*, p. 55.

Now it's time to practice positive thinking and feedback about your work. Is there a role for critical thinking? Absolutely. Is it sometimes helpful, even crucial, to have a clear-eyed gaze on where a project could be more robust, where the author could develop skill in the use of description or in creating a mesmerizing arc of story? No question. But these practices of crafting and fine-tuning are for use in the later developmental stages of our writing. The difference between Michelangelo's work as a sculptor and ours as writers is that we have no block of marble to chip away at until we string a number of words on a page! And for this work of creating marble out of thin air, profoundly positive thinking is required.

> **We'd like you now to read that piece aloud to yourself and make note:**
> **What surprises you? (specific words or phrases, images, energy)**
>   **What moves you?**
>   **What do you love about what you wrote?**
>   **What quality of your writing in general that you see reflected here has excitement or energy for you?**
> **Anything else?**

If you can't find anything you loved about what you just wrote, we can almost promise you it's not about the writing. And that's okay. Every one of our WOW facilitators has her and his own struggles with positivity. We've been well-trained, and we have agile self-protection systems in place which caution us against getting too big for our britches, getting a swelled head, getting too big in any way. As if there's something terrible about our inborn radiance.

If you didn't find anything you loved, go back through the piece and find something anyway, something you might love if you were allowed to be positive. *Fake it till you make it* is a legitimate place to begin and to continue practicing until it becomes real. We can, and do, change our brains continually, and sometimes — like right now — we can choose to change them in a powerfully positive direction.

If you assume there is goodness and value in all of your behavior, and if you consciously look for that goodness, you will see it.

> **Let's take a few minutes for three short writes: Take two or three minutes to write about something or someone it is easy for you to like. Pause.**
> **When that feels complete, choose something relatively neutral in your world – a carpet, a fork, something you don't ordinarily pay much attention to – and take time to write toward what you can genuinely like about that neutral object. Pause again.**
> **And finally, take a bit more time to write; what do your friends or loved ones like about you? Be specific about experiences, moments, actions that come to mind. Let yourself go beyond "they like me because I'm nice."**

Come back to Tara Brach's quote near the start of this chapter, and notice how it strikes you now. Notice that she uses the word *learning* — "*Learning to take in the good...*" — because she assumes that we are all innocent amateurs at this skill. We may have been taught that negativity is more intelligent and practical than positivity. This is simply untrue. We may have silenced our own voices of enthusiasm, of idealism, of love for the world, in favor of clever discernment. But this will need to change. You may congratulate yourself, for real, on your willingness to cross the threshold with us into the brave, expansive and magical practice of positivity. Really. Congratulate yourself.

10
Voice

> "It took me quite a long time to develop a voice, and now that I have it, I am not going to be silent."
>
> — Madeleine Albright

If unimpeded, energy moves naturally from vision to voice. We look across the vine-rich valley to a ridge lit by slanting afternoon sun and murmur with awe. A tender story brings a sigh. A toddler jumping in a puddle makes you chuckle. What is your own sound of outrage at the sight of police brutality, your sound at the cliff edge of ecstasy, your sound of love, sorrow, contentment, frustration?

Voice is expression, in at least two ways that matter to writers: One of these ways is in the emergence of each authentic personal voice. The other is in our quest for the voice we'll use in any given writing project. They're related, but also distinct from one another.

In our lives, we seek to express ourselves fully and with authenticity, in voices that are no one's but our own. We wail our way into the world. We giggle and gabble and learn to make words and, if all goes well, we become confident in the sounds we make. If all doesn't go well, as has been true for so many outliers and oppressed peoples, our literal voices choke on their words. Many of us cope by becoming bilingual: We learn the mainstream languages of academics or science or European English while keeping our natural languages at home, sometimes secret even from ourselves. Women's voices are routinely dismissed or silenced. Black English becomes unacceptable to white people raised in patriarchal and racist social systems.

How many of us even know what our full and authentic voices sound like? How many of us sing at the top of our lungs or howl at the moon? How often do we hear people say that they *can't* sing? What can we learn from the fact that the fear of public speaking is estimated to affect 75% of our population, with broader spread and greater intensity than the fear of death?

Most of us arrive in adulthood with, at best, adaptive versions of our own voices. And some of us hope for more than that, for the capacity to speak up out of the silence, to stand in our truth even when that truth is uncomfortable or unwelcome. Voice training of that sort is the work of creativity and courage.

As writers, we must learn to hear our own voices.

On an unusually dark Tuesday afternoon in Tuscany, clouds fall low overhead as though they will come to rest on the far hills. We gather to write and read. The mood of the group feels similarly dark, as though we too are gathering for a storm. Dulcie leads us through a visualization exercise designed to bring ourselves fully present to ourselves, our senses, our present moment. We write, it's time to read aloud, and silence prevails. No one wants to read aloud.

We enter the sacred territory of the kingdoms within, territory that doesn't yet know how to speak of itself in language we understand. We don't recognize the words that have come through us onto the page. We're embarrassed by what we found inside, by what wanted to be written. We feel ashamed of how inadequate our words are to embrace the vastness of what we would describe. Between the longing to express ourselves and the capacity to speak our deepest truths, all manner of challenges await.

Almost all of us know at least as much about impediments to voice as we do about its fruition.

I had the honor of facilitating a trauma workshop among Alaskan native women whose bloodline had been seduced by a colonizing Christian minister. They bore not only that ancestral trauma but the current wounds of sexual abuse, alcoholism, poverty, and most of all, the silencing of their voices, their language, their foundational roots. While I sat with them in a circle on the reservation in Southeast Alaska's islands, a terrible accident occurred at the docks where the island's men were loading timber for transport, and at least one man was killed. Before anyone knew how severe the damage would be, before they had any other news at all, these women fell into one another's arms. They wailed loudly and fully, wails that sounded to my ears like cries from the center of the earth itself, wails that crested and fell in waves. They did not stop until long after any European Protestant prohibitions against making a scene had surrendered entirely to the power of that archetypal sound. They cried in the pure voices of despair and loss.

As horrifying as the accident would be in their lives for a very long time to come, they would also later say that they saw their grandmothers there as they wailed. They said their voices were stronger now. They said that what happened there brought something back to them that they'd lost even as they mourned another terrible loss. These women had not, after all, entirely lost access to their channels of sound. It was desperation that brought them back to the voices of their roots.

> **Let's see how this may be for you. Consider the statement, "I am my voice, and I...." Now close your eyes, say that statement aloud, and listen for what you hear that completes the sentence. Our bodies will tell us unedited, sometimes elementary, truths. Let this voice come to the page. Write for 5 minutes.**

When I step into the exercise, I hear: "I am my voice, and I am ready." Tomorrow, I might hear something very different. My mind may comment that this doesn't make any sense or that she doesn't know what *ready* means. That's okay. This body, the place where the voice has its roots, knows something that might be worth following, exploring, and writing.

We come now to that other aspect of voice, the voice you will use in your writing project. Of course, you want that voice to be authentic. But what version of authentic? How do we find the "right" voice for any particular piece?

I started writing my first book because I had a story that felt like it would literally kill me if I did not find a way to dig it out of my bones. I joined a group in which we committed to a project we would work on for the duration. I tried to write that burning story. I kept trying. It kept going nowhere. The voice of the narrator sounded alternately distant and false with irony, as if she was pretending to know things she didn't know. As if she now understood what had happened and was condescending to tell us what she knew. This wasn't true; it also wasn't good writing.

And then, one day, the voice of the thirteen-year old girl in me woke up and wrote this: *"Snow fell from the sky in August that year. No one else saw it, but that doesn't mean it didn't happen."* I had found the voice for the book, or she had found me, and we stayed together for the duration. She is and is not *me*. Her voice is and is not *my* voice, but hers was the voice that needed to tell the story.

There may be no better way to discern the *right* voice for a piece of writing than the method I blundered into: Keep writing and keep listening. What wants expression will emerge.

> **Please try the exercise we practiced above with a character in your writing, one about whom you're curious. What do you know about his or her voice, and most notably, what does it sound like on the inside of this character? Let them say aloud, "I am my voice, and I...." Let them write for 5 minutes.**

The character I'm working with now replied, "I am my voice, and I can only say one word at a time. I press out these words through a tiny straw. But I won't stop."

We don't know how it works, and for that reason, we often call it magic. But what we know is that this is real and true: We awaken our characters perhaps more than we invent them. We let them run all over the page, and we listen to their voices.

> "I write entirely to find out what I'm thinking, what I'm looking at, what I see, and what it means. What I want and what I fear."
> — Joan Didion

> "I am large. I contain multitudes."
> — Walt Whitman

Let's acknowledge that in our beings' vast libraries, we contain an almost infinite number of voices gathered from the mirrors the world has shown us, created by experience and culture and context, voices that sometimes speak truth, are always filtered, and are sometimes wildly untrue. Sometimes we find them helpful, often not. The principle of homeostasis, alive and well in our biological systems, attempts to keep us safe by coloring within the lines. When we push against fences surrounding the known world and dare to speak of what we see in the beyond, we are bound to encounter forces that push right back. It is inevitable, then, that in a conversation about voice we will come upon impediments to creative expression, of which there may be many. Creative people in particular have encountered and taken to heart any number of skeptical voices.

One of Dulcie's first writing teachers wrote, "This is obviously the first time you've tried to write this story," a comment that stood in the way of Dulcie's writing for many years.

In eighth grade, I tried out for high school chorus. I stood in front of the piano where Miss Lewis tried a few notes, high and low, and then she asked me to sing America The Beautiful. When I did, Miss Lewis turned to me and said, "Don't ever take voice lessons." I did get into the "C" chorus in a large enough school to name their ensembles A through E, but I've never known what those words or that designation of "C" really meant. Miss Lewis' words still lodge in my throat as an inhibition. Even when it's not the intention, it's that easy to put us down.

But it's not so easy to kill a spirit, and creativity is entirely easily deterred. Obstacles are only STOP signs in the sense that at stop signs, we learn to pause, look both ways, and then continue.

We can learn to deal skillfully with internal voices who speak in opposition to our greater good. We do this not by suppressing them, but by getting to know them.

In the middle of a piece of paper, please write down the dream or the vision you've chosen to work with.

Below that dream statement, list any and all objections that come to mind. If your dream is to become a successful novelist, jot down practical objections, insecurities, skepticism, and dream-killing statements that could silence you. All of them. When you've finished this, take a full breath and let it go with a sigh. Now, above the dream statement, please counter those negations by first noting actions you could take right now toward your dream. Then, write an even stronger and more specific version of your dream statement. And finally, letting it get as big as possible, state your dream in its purest essence.

To follow these internal voices a bit further, Robin teaches writers how to face the blank page without panic in our throats. Her session, "Imaginary Dialogues: How to Use Your Inner Conversations as Springboards to Imagination," has helped writers hear multiple internal voices and get down on the page what we are hearing.

By way of introduction, she says, we all have these internal dialogues in our lives, taking the form of the clever comeback, the vital question, the one true thing you never said. This often subconscious "playlist" is gold for the writer. Honoring these dialogues can lead to opening arteries of confusion, sadness, miscommunication, jealousy, anger, or joy as the conversations find their way to the page. Robin has used this method in a number of ways: To tackle the blank page, to strengthen a scene, to understand the voice in a piece. And many, many times, she's turned to this exercise to figure out the conflict in a piece. It's a liberating form of writing, and it can be hugely informative.

Let's write.

> **Turn your attention to a dialogue that needs to happen, and take 30 minutes to write it.** *This could be a conversation in your internal life or in your character's life. It could be a way of untangling a memory or conflict you don't understand, or really, about anything that would be interesting for you to hear about from two different points of view. Try to hear and to express the specific voices of the players: Is his a raspy voice, a pressured way of speaking? Is she speaking directly or lyrically? Do they speak with a Maine accent? Transcribe, without editing, what you hear in your head. Embrace the interior monologues that only you can write, and only you can decipher. It can be magical.*

As can be helpful after each of your writing practices in this book, read your words aloud. Notice what strikes you. Notice how it feels to have written that conversation.

Dulcie struggled with converting the tangle of visions that played regularly in her mind's eye into stories that would make sense and be meaningful to others. She'd begin her story with two or three reasonable characters experiencing their lives in somewhat conventional ways. The characters would meet over coffee or at the gym or a school conference. And then, regardless of her intention for the story's plot, at least one of the characters would begin to show signs of nuttiness. The pages filled with blurts of nonsensical phrases, repetitive obsessive behaviors, characters talking to people who weren't there. Nothing seemed to be off-limits. "There they go again," she would come to say, and the story would end up being another vignette about growing up with a crazy mother.

Dulcie didn't want to write that story. She'd lived that story, and she was done with it. She wanted to write fiction and, *if you don't mind,* she'd say, *I'd like to write a story where no one has to go off the deep end,* but the answer seemed to be No. Suppression does not foster either truth or creativity.

So, she wrote *Confessions of a Therapist,* a book that included stories from that childhood she'd

lived and linked them to clients' narratives from her years of private therapy practice. Instead of making up sane people to inhabit her stories, she let real people speak in their real voices, in ways that brought warmth and grief and humor and clarity to the lives of her clients and herself. It was as though the visions in her head would not move on until they'd had their voices heard, until their dialogues were complete.

Back in Tuscany on this stormy afternoon, Dulcie takes the lead and reads her bare and tender writing from the morning's exercise. As rain pours down from the heavens, we draw in closer. We speak, we listen, we recognize in one another's words the echoes of our own barely acknowledged thoughts.

Australian aboriginal peoples walked the land and sang the songs of their journeys, songs which are to this day followed – literally followed – by their descendants who track these songlines across the land on vision quests. Their songs become the GPS instructions of the natural world. That's how powerful our voices genuinely are. Vision becomes voice becomes map becomes reality, if only we can learn to speak and listen to those deepest truths.

11
At Home in the Body

"And the world cannot be discovered by a journey of miles, no matter how long, but only by a spiritual journey, a journey of one inch, very arduous and humbling and joyful, by which we arrive at the ground at our feet, and learn to be at home."
— Wendell Berry

September mornings in Tuscany begin with a slight chill in the air. It's fleece weather, espresso weather. I'm sitting on my sun-colored yoga mat on the brick patio, temporarily in shadow. Music wings softly on the air. With yoga mats and blankets, people walk down the hill and up from the coffee machines. Some of us are bright-eyed, some of us drowsy, and some of us turn over in bed and snooze. It's early. On every morning of the retreat, yoga arises from the silence and the wisps of dreams. Every morning we're glad we did it.

But why do we do this? And what does yoga have to do with writing? Many of WOW's participants come to our retreats because they long to live for a few days or a lifetime in the integration of body and mind, in yoga and writing. But the idea of yoga is not met with universal enthusiasm. Some of us are wary of the imagined yoga class of perfect bodies, perfect alignment, and perfect yoga outfits. Others conjure images of Indian yogis, foot behind neck, eyes rolled to the heavens, standing on one leg. We can find it hard to arrive in our bodies. We can find it hard to locate ourselves in the culturally created stories of what yoga is and why we practice.

I know differently. There is room for all of us on the yoga mat. Over the years, I've recommended yoga to many of my psychotherapy clients, and for those who took to it, the practice has been a powerful tool of support.

For writers, a yoga practice can be even more important, because we do not write with our minds. Every thought or sensation or feeling or curiosity that forms in the far reaches of the rhinencephalon or the amygdala has to find expression through our bodies. How easy to forget! Look at this group of writers: We hunch over notebooks, curl around computers and phones, we sit for hours unmoving. You might think by looking at us that there is no place for the life of the body in the writer's life. But please, don't think that. We believe the two are inseparable.

Yoga will be our focus in this chapter, and yoga is the physical practice we recommend for retreat participants. But we don't assume it is the only suitable path. Other forms of exercise may compel you more, and that's okay. One reason we bring our bodies to our writing is to periodically step aside or get ahead of our minds, to allow our bodies to arrive at internal spaces uncluttered with used words and dusty thoughts. Something happens in the spaces that open up during and after exercise. New thoughts form. Inspiration becomes possible when there's room for it to flex and stretch.

As a form of exercise, yoga invites us not to outrun thoughts or to join with other rhythms, but to *step in*. Breath and presence become elixirs for stress reduction, relief from obsessive thoughts, mood enhancement, clarity of mind, and creativity, along with physical and emotional strength and flexibility. We practice not to feel anything in particular but to *drop in* to the experience of letting body, breath and mind wake up to one another and to draw a line of words from that waking to wherever your being wants you to go. Yoga as prompt.

Take a deep breath, and let it go with a sigh. Do this again, and pause. Notice anything at all.

Often with this simplest of actions, breath with intention and attention, something changes. We notice sounds around us or stillness within. The present moment expands, the list of chores diminishes. Wild mind circles and starts to settle ever so slightly, almost unnoticeably perhaps. Let that be enough. The word yoga literally means *yoke*, the yoke of body and mind and spirit. If the yoga you practice is as pure and uncomplicated as the breathwork we just created together, that is without question still yoga.

Sweep your arms up to the sky and let them float gently down. Do this one time without breathing. Notice what you notice. Now sweep your arms up on a big inhale and let them float down on an exhale. Any difference? One more time, sweep your arms up to the sky, this time as if you are reaching toward the heavens with your greatest longing. Pause there, and then as your arms float down, let sunlight and sky and the answer to your longing gather around you. Bring your hands to your heart, one on top of the other, close your eyes and breathe.

Movement. Breath. Intention. Metaphor. The shapes we make with our yoga bodies are intentional and wise, exquisitely designed over thousands of years to accomplish particular changes in our beings. Although its practice in the West can mimic any other fitness class, in yoga we're invited to bring fitness together with presence in a more holistic experience. It is *your* presence and *your* body that contain the wisdom to practice your yoga, your movement, your breath, your intentions.

One of our favorite yoga teachers, Tanya Witman, reports that the more advanced she becomes as a yoga practitioner and teacher, the less she does! A class with Tanya can move exquisitely slowly, breath by breath, subtle movements building on one another. Students find themselves doing things they did not think they could do, expanding in ways their bodies do not otherwise expand, and appreciating the power of subtlety.

When tension is high, you might find that the opposite of subtlety is right for you and that a fast-paced, breath-filled series of movements and sounds is what your body most wants. The memoirist Dani Shapiro, a long-time yogini, heads for her mat when she's come to a place in her writing where she has to step away and clear the mental palate. It's a great idea. So is starting the day with yoga, a kind of pre-clearing!

Just as we practice writing during a retreat with the hope that it will become a regular practice, we come to yoga or our forms of mindful physical practices hoping that these will become everyday rituals. Regularity makes us reliable. Becoming trustworthy to ourselves opens us to our depths and to the Muse of writers who flies over the earth looking for a receptive place to land. It's helpful if our bodies are reliably in place when the Muse flies by.

Lynn goes to her yoga mat every day, even if it's the kind of day when all she can do is lie on the mat and breathe. I keep my mat open on the floor as an invitation and reminder of a space and time apart yet always available. We can forget so quickly to do the things we most love to do.

Focus. Patience. Presence. Increasing awareness of subtlety. Reliability. Commitment. Tension release. Stretch, strength, flexibility. Integration and rest.

Not every human body loves the feelings that accompany a practice like yoga. Many of us have bodies that hurt when we move, and many of us hold in our bodies the memories of violation or violence. By the time we have lived a few decades on the earth, enough pain may have happened that the habit of avoiding the body's messages can be a well-worn groove. If this in any way describes your relationship to your body, please be kind to yourself. If yoga for you means several minutes of breathing, if yoga for you means tears falling on your mat, if yoga for you means ever so gently approaching sensations of pain and taking a breath there, let that be enough.

Interestingly enough, exercise for fitness can also become a way of avoiding the body's subtler signals as we make ourselves strong. If you're an avid athlete, may we suggest that you approach this particular practice slowly? Take time to notice how it feels to be *in* this body rather than *working on* your body. Compassionate noticing is the writer's way.

Stop reading now, and take your body out for exercise. *If you don't have a yoga practice you like, invent one or look for online classes. If you don't have a music playlist you love, make one or steal from friends' and teachers' Spotify lists. Take at least 20 minutes to move. Set an intention for this practice or this moment in your life (Openness, Flow, Presence, Kindness, or Strength, for example). Let your movement be fluid. Let yourself be present to your signals more than to any other instruction. Go at your own pace, noticing your body's natural inclinations — does it want to begin slowly or quickly, to move subtly or expansively? Let this flow have a beginning, middle, and end. Consider awakening, quickening, arriving, returning, and rest. We are composed of ever-changing natural rhythms. Explore and experiment with your rhythms. Without being hard on yourself, consider trying something you haven't tried before. Take care of yourself, and don't push farther than your edge. At the same time, let yourself go toward that edge, that place where sensation meets discomfort, and go no farther. Notice what you notice there.*

Come to rest, letting awareness drift and sensations fall back to stillness. While your consciousness settles and without effort, let your body do what it does best. And then, when the rest feels complete, let's write.

For this writing, use as a prompt any experience you had in the movement practice. *You may notice that the most powerful experience you had was a physical one — that tight hamstring, the opening of your chest. On the other hand, your thoughts and emotions may have been more notable for their wildness, their commentary on your practice or your general worthiness, their refusal to focus, or their soft surrender to a delightful moment. Write that. When you feel your pen or your fingers slowing down or pausing, follow the original sensation or thought or emotion back in time: Where in my life did I first feel this, think this? What is my story of tightness? Of opening? What is my story of yoga?*

Read your writing aloud. Note what particularly stands out to you. Note where the power and charge of the writing are most potent. Pat yourself on the back. Bow to yourself, your fellow writers and seekers, and the Muse who paused to spend these moments with you. Tell her you'll be back.

Sun streams across the patio, one lone bird sways in the top branches of the Lebanon cedar, breakfast sounds call to us from the dining pergola below, and we emerge from yoga space both subtly changed and more fully ourselves. Whatever you just did, whether your time in your body was restful or invigorating, soothing or agitating, let's call it yoga, that yoke between body and mind and spirit, our most direct channel to creativity.

12
Heart

> "Earth is crammed with heaven."
> — Rob Brezsny

We come now to the heart of the matter. As with the heart chakra in Eastern traditions, the physical heart lives at the center of the body, and love is at the center of that center. As with all creativity, writing lives on love.

Energetically, our bodies' heart space forms the nexus of connection between our spirits (inspiration, intuition, dream, and vision) and our bodies (feeling, sensation, movement, and manifestation). Devotion, compassion, rhythm, and connection are the language of the heart, and love is their energetic footprint.

Devotion

> "Safety is not the absence of threat. It is the presence of connection."
> — Gabor Mate

Whether we're writing romance novels drenched with sentiment or essays about climate change or stories from an American childhood, whether we're just beginning to describe ourselves as writers or we've been coming to the page for a lifetime, we've got to love what we're doing. And it helps if we know something of what it is we love about it.

Because writing is hard. Ernest Hemingway, among others, is credited with saying, "Writing is easy. All you do is stare at a blank sheet of paper until drops of blood form on your forehead." Writing asks for vision and courage and willpower. It asks for commitment. It asks for action in the form of moving inchoate images into concrete words on a page. There are going to be things you don't like about the work of writing. I don't like the pressure I feel about writing when I'd rather go swimming. Until I do it, I don't like the feeling of having to jump into the fire of authentic vulnerability. I don't like the logistics of moving work from page to publisher. But I also know that I don't like *not* writing even more. And so, it is remembering and reviving what I love about it that keeps me coming back.

You don't start out writing good stuff. You start out writing crap and thinking it's good stuff, and then gradually you get better at it. That's why I say one of the most valuable traits is persistence."

— Octavia Butler

The persistence of discipline? Yes, maybe. But devotion? Absolutely. What is it to which we are devoted enough to keep coming back? It may be for you that the work of writing itself doesn't light your fire. Often what stirs the heart is the story, the one that whispers and calls to you, the story that is only yours to tell. Or it is your love for your partner, your newest grandchild, the loss of a parent, that brings you to the page? Love takes many forms, and love moves mountains.

So let's start there. **Write for at least 10 minutes, completing the sentence, "What I love about writing is…" If that doesn't speak to you, write to this prompt: What do I love enough (what matters enough to me) to want to write it?**

Within each of us, beyond the reach of the habitual self, lives another deeper self suffused with the radiance of the heart. You know this is true. This deeper self is the dwelling place of your writer, the home of your creative fire. Yes, writing is hard; but so is birth. And writing is birthed by faith, fidelity, and, above all, devotion. Love.

The heart always speaks the language of connection, of relationship. The first relationship, the bond we form within us between spirit and body, forms when we allow ourselves to be *who we are*. We come to the page and write those words that are welling up inside, not the words we think we *should* be writing, but the words that are whispering or yelling or cajoling at the heart's door. The words that melt us. When we do it again and again, we demonstrate that we can be trusted, that our devotion is reliable, and that the heart is safe with us.

You should write because you love …"

— Annie Proulx

The heart speaks in images, in colors, in body sensations, and sometimes in shorthand. The heart says, I hate this. That hurts. I am afraid. That feels wonderful. Like a Zen koan designed to short circuit our rational thinking, heart language makes phrases that might make little sense to the mind and yet can be fully felt. The heart makes connections between sight and sound, between smell and touch. The heart says, skin like moonlight, freckles torn from her mother's hands, grief cracking her bones. All the senses tumble in with one another, and the heart does this out of love. It just can't help *connecting*.

Connection within and connection between. In some often buried place inside, we long for that experience of being close enough to one another that we can be completely known. Joni Mitchell mourned that she and a lover could get so "close to the skin and the bone... and still feel so alone, and still feel related." And isn't that how it is to be living in a human body with a heart made of timelessness and longing? We don't often or reliably get what we most deeply want. And yet, in every which way we know how, we try. As writers, we reach toward perfect union by doing our best to make our readers *feel* what we feel. We fall in love with a man or a woman or a waterfall or a quality of light, a soaring musical interlude or a saturation of color. The heart pours itself out into the world in the language of connection, in the form of love.

This is where creativity takes form and flight.

> Let a joy keep you...Smashed to the heart Under the ribs With a terrible love. Joy always, Joy everywhere— Let joy kill you! Keep away from the little deaths.."
>
> — Carl Sandburg

Please write a love letter to yourself. Make as little sense as possible but use as many senses as possible, and mix them up if you can. Let your heart speak.

Now take a look back at the *inspiration*, at the *dream* you discovered in the earlier chapters of this book, and specifically look for the love there. You've likely dreamt of something that takes your vision out beyond the borders of yourself, out beyond the money you'd like to make or the fame or appreciation you seek. Your big *dream* is likely in some way of benefit to others. If it isn't, if you find that you've spoken of more self-oriented goals, you may not have gone quite far enough toward naming that bigger dream. We are so much bigger than we know. Our hearts long to connect with the whole entire world.

Compassion

As writers, the devotional quality of the heart brings us to the page. But there's more. The compassionate quality of the heart deepens our understanding of the world and these beings we want to write about.

> All I ever wanted was to reach out and touch another human being not just with my hands but with my heart."
>
> — Tahereh Mafi

A successful novelist writes page-turning books about Christianity's mysteries, iconic churches and the forces that oppose them. These novels are great fun to read. And yet, to the eye of the heart, something is missing: It is difficult to care about any of his characters. Perhaps this author cares deeply about buildings and history and not so much for humans. Perhaps as a result the something missing is a feel for human connection. To judge by the remarkable sales history of anything he writes, this is not a deal-breaker for success. But we're interested here in going deeper, into the wilder and more mysterious world of loving what is alive.

To write with *compassion* about others, we have to dig deep into understanding them. Our surface judgments about them, however accurate or long-held, will not help. And in order to dig deep into understanding others, we have to be willing to meet them with humility, with some degree of self-understanding, and with at least a bit of what the Buddhist teacher Tara Brach terms "radical acceptance." Acceptance that they are as human as you and I, acceptance that they've come to be who they are in the same blundering and unconscious ways that you and I have arrived in ourselves. Acceptance that "there but for the grace of God, go I..." As we write toward understanding the world through the eyes and the nose and the heart of an Other, we are engaged in the work of deep democracy, of creative oneness. And this is not purely a moralistic or aspirational truth: If we do not do this work, if we create characters who behave like caricatures of themselves, our readers and we will find them boring.

> "Write about the emotions you fear the most."
> — Laurie Halse Anderson

We believe that the deeper we go, the more we are alike. In a process a bit like what the Velveteen Rabbit teaches us, writing with compassion toward the inner depths makes both us and our characters more real. If we ourselves don't go deep, our characters forever swim in the shallows.

Let's try this.

> **Turn to a character in your landscape — perhaps a character from your life or lineage — who you've experienced as negative in any way. Give him or her a voice. Listen to the quality of the voice, age, gender, appearance, clothing, demeanor, posture, anything you can get hold of that fleshes out this character in your mind's eye.** There may be more than one of these characters, in which case you may want to choose one for this exercise and come back later to meet and greet another! The negative voices of our lives tend not to expire until we give them breathing room and allow them to grow and change along with the rest of us. So, they're easy to find.
>
> **Now, let this character speak. Listen to him or her on the page** with all the compassion you can muster. Where was she born, what happened that shaped her, wounded or frightened him, what do they struggle with? And most importantly, what does she or he need? Let them tell you all about how they came to be. Let yourself be the scribe for this crucial character. When judgment creeps in, engage compassion. Seek to understand.
>
> Pause. Rest. Read this writing aloud. Feel any internal shift that may have happened as a result of your attempt to understand.

Rhythm

For writers, at least one more aspect of the heart directly affects our work, and that is *rhythm*.

Our physical hearts create the rhythm of our lives. Soothed by the sound of mother's heartbeat in the womb before we even arrive on the planet, we imprint to that sound, that beat, that foundational rhythm. Particularly when we read out loud, we notice at a subtle level when a piece is gratifying rhythmically, and we notice when it throws us off. We can use this awareness to support us as we write.

Pam listened to a beautiful chant that lifted her spirits and soothed her mind until she heard a phrase made of words that seemed too long or too bulky to fit inside the space that was there for it.

Something in her noticed the rhythmic change and balked at it. Rhythm can propel us forward as it resonates with internal beats, or it can, like chalk on a blackboard, throw us off.

We think of rhythm as being the property of poetry and music. But there's more. Like the heartbeat behind all our experiences, we hear the heartbeat of a prose piece behind the words, feel its rhythm as satisfying, satiating, aggravating, harsh, exciting, ecstatic. What is the rhythm of fear? Of contentment? How might these emotions be conveyed by rhythm alone?

Explore your rhythms.

How does your writing respond to Beethoven? To Adele? To indigenous drum music? Try it.

Rhythm is the literal language of the heart. Rhythm is what moves the heart, and thus the blood, through our bodies, our relationships, our lives. We need to move our bodies, and we need to move them in rhythm. Left, right, left, right, left, right, thoughts begin to order themselves. Breath in, breath out, spider webs of complication blow away, and breath in, breath out, we create space for what will come next. We align ourselves with our hearts' beat, that steady pulse of aliveness, and watch our writing come alive as well.

"A word after a word after a word is power."

— Margaret Atwood

Devote yourself to the practice of writing and to the story that needs to be told. Develop great compassion toward self and other. Let your heart melt, rage, flood, burst, and fall on to the page.

13
Play

"You need chaos in your soul to give birth to a dancing star."

— Nietzsche

It's time for a break.

We've been sitting in marginally comfortable iron and cloth chairs under the shade of the pergola for the better part of four days – or at the desk in the back room or on a stool at the kitchen counter – and we've been disciplined, even devoted. We've brought our big dreams and our visions. We've opened again and again to some of our most essential creative truths. Some of you have named a particular project you're working on. Others have found you're more interested in the simple and hardly easy process of developing a writing *practice*. We hope you're discovering wonderful things about writing and yourself. There's more to come.

But now, it's time to play.

Play in the fields of imagination brings air and light and inspiration to the earnest effort of writing. The importance of this can't be minimized. If our work is to be regenerative, it's essential that we regularly break away from the work of writing in order to feed and clothe that writing with beauty, with fresh breezes, with spontaneous pleasure. We need to lift our heads up from the page in order to let life in!

> "Creativity represents a miraculous coming together of the uninhibited energy of the child with its apparent opposite and enemy, the sense of order imposed by the disciplined adult intelligence."
>
> — Norman Podhoretz

Like the Artist's Date Julia Cameron recommends, we are strong proponents of taking play dates often. Play is what we do for no practical purpose but the enjoyment of the activity itself. Play is not for cultural enrichment, not for checking off the boxes of betterment activities we should be undertaking. Play is about the simple joy of having no agenda other than that of following wonder and curiosity wherever they may go. Sadly, many of us set down our playthings when we became adults. Becoming rational, purposeful and responsible was important, and looking like a grownup mattered for job interviews and self-esteem, for fundamental life-skills and for raising children. But what if both aspects of our beings could thrive within us?

As the weight of the world grew heavy on her, I know a woman who stopped singing, stopped dancing, and then stopped listening to music entirely. When children sway and twirl and leap at the music of a Celtic band at a summer fair, their parents rarely join in. Why don't adults sit for the face-painting activity at the same summer fair? Why don't we all take regular time to indulge in color or movement or rhythm or beauty? What, really, could be more important? Playfulness flings the doors open to the Muse.

Honestly, I had to work at it. On a weeklong retreat for Adult Children of Alcoholics, we all had to work at it. "Go and play today," the group leaders instructed. "Together." We grimaced at one another. This was a more challenging instruction than working on our trauma or taking accountability for our actions. We were there to work. But we went for a walk. Someone snuck off the path and hid behind a tree. Play happened, and I'm glad there is no record of the awkwardness and the silliness of our attempts to be silly. I felt better, though. I think we all did. Why did this matter? Why does it matter to us as creatives? Because closing the doors on our spontaneity invites all manner of other deaths to what is vital.

Dulcie takes herself to the movies. She goes to a card store and buys cards she likes and then goes to a coffee shop and writes them out and sends them to herself and people who pop into her mind. She goes for a walk that she usually goes on but acts like she's a different person than the person who typically goes on this walk. She's an eight-year old boy, or she's someone from Egypt or Venus.

Robin loves picnics. On a blanket under a 100-year-old tree, she looks up through its proud limbs and listens to the wind moving the leaves, watches it chase the clouds. Wind, she believes, is a whisper from the gods.

If like some of the rest of us, you aren't as comfortable with play as you are with purposeful work, we can promise you that your artist knows how to play and craves more of that! And we can also promise you that with practice, you'll get better at it too.

During our Tuscany retreats, the week thus far has been pretty intense. We come to Wednesday afternoons off with various feelings, including the feeling of being a bit wrung out by all the collective input and all the creative outpouring. What each person needs for their time off will differ. Naps. Pool time. Long walks. Shopping. Alone time to write on their projects. Casual time with new friends.

We encourage checking in with yourself to notice what will feel like rest and recreation at this point. Re-creation is as essential to a writer as putting words on a page, because no one can write from an empty well. Do what you want and don't do what you don't want. Think of this time as feeding your artist, who needs to dream a lazy afternoon dream or run her hand through silk scarves in the doorway of a store. To take photographs of hummingbirds or pick grapes from the vine and brush the Nebbiolo clouds off their skins. To ride a red scooter with the dry Italian wind blowing away any cares.

If you're initially at a loss, remember what you loved as a child. Did you lie on the ground watching clouds? Did you draw pictures of the sun and flowers with giant petals? Did you build mud-houses or towers of blocks? Did you ride your bike, wind blowing through your hair? What did you purely enjoy?

Try it.

A bit of science may help you to jump wildly around your living room or to get out your paints. A principle of task mastery from learning theory states that "practice that emerges out of enthusiastic play lays down habits of discipline that endure."[6] An accompanying principle is that if celebration or recognition of some kind doesn't accompany new learning, learning is less likely to continue expanding.

After a writing session on a WOW retreat, we play music, and if we're so inspired, we move around. Sometimes that music is meditative and heartful. Sometimes it brings us to the madness of pure energetic release. Sometimes we play the Dixie Chicks, *Wide Open Spaces*, because "Who doesn't know what I'm talking about; who's never left home, who's never set out...?" Most of us find that after we've scraped out the insides of our minds and memories to write, there's plenty of excess physical energy that wants expression. This is how alcohol and cigarettes and overeating have long lived in writers' lives, and this is where giving our beings even better ways to express ourselves can become powerful and welcome practices.

When you've worked hard enough and it's time to play, the possibilities are vast. If your playfulness needs physical expression, put on some music. We hungrily gather music from every source that moves us, and we begin to discover which pieces might be right for any given moment. You may already have your favorite jumping around songs, your favorite tug at your heartstrings music, your fierce busting out jams. If you do, and if you haven't yet gathered these songs together, make a playlist for after-writing. Call it *After Glow*. Call it *Even Wider Open*. Call it a good idea. And then, move around. Move with the feeling of a character who's struggling in your writing. Move with the tenderness of a kind mother who cares about you and the hard work you're doing. Move like you're shaking off every bit of energy that doesn't belong to you, as if you're making room for exactly what you have dreamed of creating in your life. Move really, really slowly. Jump around at

---

[6] Hallowell, *Superparenting for ADD*.

hyper speed. Hunt like a jaguar. There's no right way to do this; which means there's no wrong way to do it other than not to do it, because what doesn't move, doesn't move. You can move around for the length of one song or many. Bring curiosity and kindness to this brave and beautiful being whose body you inhabit.

    Your playfulness may take an entirely different form. My sister never jumped around in her life as far as I know; her play was in the world of color and lines. One of my friends marks the walls of his house with Sharpie cartoon characters. Tree-climbing is time-honored play. Cooking something new and strange, making bird houses, singing in the woods, trying on clothes. Remember, play is defined not by *what* we do, but about the *spirit* in which we do it.

    Take a break. Play. Do what once came naturally, and watch it become natural again. Do what you want, for its own sake, and make it a regular practice.

And then, if you'd like a writing prompt, here's one. **Write something ridiculous, something you'd never otherwise write. A limerick. An advertising jingle. A porn scene. Bring together two "characters" — a banana and a mongoose? — who might otherwise never meet. Loosen it up. Write like someone else, with an accent. You get the idea.**

14
Getting (What's in the Way) Out of the Way

"Fear is a natural reaction to moving closer to the truth."
— Pema Chodron

After Tuscany's mid-week sightseeing and writing time and naps, we return to the farm and the pergola on the hill as the sun sends her last rays across the valleys. We're more comfortable with one another now, more likely to bust out a dance move or tell a secret or laugh louder than we have in years. We're ready to go deeper. We're ready to let our writing drop down through the layers of accumulated voices - the voice we "should" write with, the "nice" voice, the "appropriate" voice - in search of living, breathing stories that can stand up for themselves.

Beyond this point, there be dragons. Medieval map-makers drew symbols on their charts to indicate territories of danger, or more accurately, territories that hadn't yet been explored. Dragons. But dragons are mythical, made in the minds of humans. In order to protect us, our hard-wired brains imagine danger in the *beyond,* which we then create rules and rituals and structures to avoid.

We've passed the midpoint in our writing retreat on the journey between inspiration and manifestation, and we find ourselves in a place we've never been before. Do we imagine dragons here? Do we have what we need to go on?

At some point, your light of inspiration may dim in the shadow of entirely predictable and necessarily navigable obstacles on the path. *Predictable and navigable obstacles.* We don't know of a writer who slides by undeterred. But we all know of writers who navigate successfully, who emerge in the world with their work, their devotion, and their inspiration still shining bright.

This chapter will take you through some of the difficult spaces that might otherwise stand in your way. It's a longer chapter than some of the others: Potential obstacles on the way to writing success are many and varied. By way of responding to these, we offer a smorgasbord of tools and approaches, some of which may appeal greatly to you while others may not. We encourage you to take your time with the practices, to take this chapter in smaller bites if that feels appropriate. Take breaks, move your body, breathe, play. And try all the exercises if you can. Persistence is a skill in itself.

> Successful writers are not the ones who write the best sentences. They are the ones who keep writing. They are the ones who discover what is most important and strangest and most pleasurable in themselves, and keep believing in the value of their work, despite the difficulties."
>
> — Bonnie Friedman, *Writing Past Dark.*

In the above quote, Bonnie Friedman gives voice to the single most essential practice of every writer: *Keep writing.*

But the guardians, critics, fears, and anxious entities who wring their hands in despair or stand over us with pursed lips and pointing fingers do not always make that possible, let alone easy. While the most frequent obstacles to *getting it done* take a variety of shapes and forms, they are essentially made up of fear and its companion, shame. Do any of these sound familiar to you?

I don't know enough.
It isn't good enough.
I'm not good enough.
There's no room in the world for this story. (Either: It's been told before or, No one is going to be interested.)
What will my family think?
What if people judge me?
I'm stuck: I don't know how to decide what to do next.
I don't have the time. The space. The money.
I'm going to be revealed as a big fake.

Fear gives us compelling reasons to stay on the safe side, to step back from the page. It's understandable. Often the most talented among us are also the most sensitive, the most burdened by anxiety, the ones for whom the requirements to edit or listen to critique or manage rejection can swamp the outpouring of our creativity.

When we set out to write something that *matters,* it's not only the fear of rejection that slows the pen, but the fact that writing stirs fires in the depths. Writing goes against the rules. Writing asks us not to stay safe but to jump into the fire. We may fear that there is nothing inside of any worth, or that what we would write is so explosive that it will destroy worlds. We fear we might burn or fall apart or in some other way be unable to *handle* the story we feel compelled to tell. Our carefully constructed identities fear they will not survive the emergence of truth.

And then, like the medieval map-makers, we unconsciously create structures to keep us safe. We distract ourselves. We prioritize other peoples' needs. We remind ourselves that the world has been just fine without our words. We stop writing.

If you are among the sensitive or the anxious or the untamed or the magical or the depressed, if you recognize any of the phrases above, you are welcome here, where we aim to share what we've learned about turning obstacles into opportunities. We believe the spark that calls you to write is eminently worthwhile. We are confident that opening again and again to your creativity is what will keep you fully alive. Fully. Alive. Sometimes that will hurt. Sometimes it will make you soar.

Just as the many faces of obstacles may all in fact be expressions of fear, the many practices for encountering those obstacles essentially arise from love. Let's dive in.

> Perhaps it is just as well to be rash and foolish for a while. If writers were too wise, perhaps no books would get written at all. It might be better to ask yourself, 'Why?' afterward than before. Anyway, the force of somewhere in space which commands you write in the first place, gives you no choice. You take up the pen when you are told, and write what is commanded."
>
> — Zora Neale Hurston

"I just wrote this."

The most straightforward principle for working with internal critique of any kind is to realize that the writer and the critics within us are separate characters. They operate with different skill sets, appetites, risk tolerances, and even with different bedtimes. The writer, as if a younger sibling, may need our protection. But these characters are all family and therefore must coexist with as much harmony as possible.

Wide Open Writing doesn't focus on editing during our group retreats because we're dedicated to peaceful coexistence between writer and editor. When we're writing in a generative way, we remind one another that we're not editing, not yet. This means that we also don't encourage – or even allow! — self-deprecating, disempowering clarifications. You're probably familiar with these: "I didn't really write what I meant to write here..", "I didn't follow the instructions," "I hate what I wrote..." When we read aloud, only one disclaimer is allowed: "I just wrote this."

However, we do make time in Tuscany and our other retreats for participants to meet individually with facilitators. In those sessions we talk about anything that matters, whether it's a particular kind of editing question or a general concern about the writing life. That's where we may offer suggestions about how to work with a thorny writing problem. That's where, when asked, we might get out the red pencil.

Delays and obstructions are commonplace when we're attempting to do something different. And in fact, we can measure the importance of the new thing we're trying to do by the size of the force that rises to block it! We would like to support you in doing it anyway. Every successful writer has found ways of evading, skirting, distracting, tricking, persuading, or manipulating obstacles sufficiently to allow the

authentic voice to emerge. Not perfectly, but enough. We want you to have those tools.

A playful way of encountering and moving beyond a disruptive obstacle is to **exaggerate it physically.** Give it shape and sound, make it into the most absurd form of itself, let it walk around and declare things, let it drool or growl or become a formless blob, and make it cartoon-like. Let it become silly enough that at some point, you recognize the voice for what it is, a little robot of a voice that no longer serves you. Maybe you will try this with the character of a particularly tenacious obstacle. What does "None of this matters!" look like in its cartoon form?

And then there's **bowing.** When the long shadow of a self-doubting voice comes to call, some of us learn to turn and bow. "Thank you," we say, "for your passion about this project. Thank you for your help. I will definitely want to hear more from you. And right now I'm just writing." Even our inner critics want to be honored, and they tend to behave well when they are treated with respect.

The effectiveness of any of the strategies we're suggesting in this chapter may depend on the nature of the obstacle. Most important to remember is that when it comes to overseeing our reality, we are more powerful and creative than we know! Just because a voice is screaming at you, just because that voice screaming at you sounds a lot like an adult who taught you that you're powerless, doesn't mean you're powerless. Your intention is everything.

Chod

The most powerful and creative practice we can employ to work with our internal obstacles is also the most ancient: *Personification,* and its partner, *Chod.* We'll start with getting more familiar with personification of the "demons" who haunt our thoughts. Then we'll introduce the Buddhist practice of *Chod*, also known as *Feed Your Demons*, described in more detail in Tsultrim Allione's excellent book by the same name, and based on principles of compassion and care as powerful healers. It's a practice with several parts to it, so it will be helpful to read through the entire prompt before returning to the beginning to experience it yourself.

> As a follow-up to the compassion exercise in Chapter 12, sit for a few minutes letting yourself feel the presence of some part of yourself who doesn't fully support your best self-expression. This presence might be a thought form, as in "I don't have anything special to offer." Or it might be experienced as a personal quality, rigidity or timidity, impatience or difficulty making decisions. It might be a feeling state - anxiety or depression. Where in your body does this "demon" live? What's the whole feel of his/her/its energy? What sensations accompany its presence? Is it a bellyache, a dull headache, a feeling in your chest or your arms? Just notice.
>
> Let yourself imagine that this demon takes form and becomes a whole fleshed-out being, perhaps sitting across from you. Maybe this being is a blob of goo, a rusty pile of metal, a relative or an ancestor, a teacher, a character who comes to you entirely from imagination and intuition. Spend some moments getting the feel of this being.
>
> Now that the personification process has sunk in a bit, we engage the practice of Chod to feed the demon and watch it transform. Do not worry if you feel like you haven't yet found a form for this demon: It may come during the remainder of the practice. We've found that it's helpful to practice with eyes closed but with a journal nearby for notes, drawings, and thoughts that arise.
>
> As if the demon is sitting right in front of you, ask her/him, "What do you need? If you can move to another seat, change places with the demon and let yourself enter its skin and its awareness. Listen inside for the demon's answer to the question you've asked. If the answer that emerges is reactive ("I need you to shut up." "I need you to do what I say." "I need you to be more responsible."), ask again, "What do you really need?" Go on with this until you "hear" an answer that rings true as if from a place below which there is no further depth. After you've heard what the demon needs, please return to your seat.
>
> Now, turn yourself entirely into the essence of what your demon has told you that she/he needs. Take a moment to imagine this essence, its color, its texture, its heat or coolness, and then begin to feed that essence to your demon until something changes. Your essence may take the form of a quality of light, a tincture or syrup, a soup or a breeze, or something else. Feeding might be by spoon or touch or as a bath in sparkling water or a golden syrup poured from above. Whatever it takes. When you've done this for a while, a new version of the demon might show itself to you, one who has changed shape or size or attitude. At that point, you may pause the feeding.
>
> From your seat, ask this changed demon, who now may have a new name, "Will you be my ally?" If the answer is "Yes," please ask, "What will you do for me?" Listen.
>
> Look for opportunities. Even the most powerful internal demons have great potential to grow and change, and in this respect, they can become powerful helpers in our lives.
>
> Rest for a few minutes in awareness of the shifting inner landscape. Notice how you feel on the inside. Bring this story to your writing.

My demon, formed of the feeling of being too sensitive to withstand the hard edges of the world, took the shape of a skinless Gollum-like creature who huddled in corners and under rocks. The ally that emerged as I worked with feeding that demon what it thought it needed - warmth, cushioning, and comfort - still had no skin but was electric with radiance. How could that ally help me, I asked? By representing and reminding me of my powerful connection to Energy in its purest form. That kind of strength.

Chod is an all-purpose practice you can call on repeatedly to work with recurring demons and new ones as they show up, which they will do. The more we practice care and compassion toward our internal doubters and dream-killers, the less desperate and disruptive they become. They do not stop coming, as far as we know, but they do change. We find ourselves working more and more deeply through our healing from old beliefs we've carried for too long. Chod is also a practice you can use as you write toward understanding a character in your writing. What demons plague her? What do they need? How can they help the character's journey?

Will

Now that you've spent a little time with demons and allies, you may have found that under their protective layers, most demons feel powerless and under-served, while our allies come bearing many forms of strength as their gifts.

The archetypal feminine practice of *Chod* is one we've found to be most helpful for the deepest work of encountering obstacles, but without doubt our *will* has more than a walk-on part in moving from dream to manifestation. Energies connected with core strength live in the soft center of the front of our bodies. If you engage your core belly muscles and hold them there for a moment or two now, you might feel connected with that strong central energy.

In *The Teachings of Don Juan* by Carlos Castaneda, a shamanic teacher leaps from shore to a rock in the middle of an impossibly wide stream. He does this by sending out waves of power from his solar plexus, waves which take hold of the rock that is his goal before the rest of his body simply follows. This is the true nature of that power center we all carry in the middle of us, intention given focus and will. Core energy brings fire and focus to the aspiration that drives us. But in fact, many of us collapse at the middle as we go through our days, thereby diminishing or even cutting off the power that sources us. Notice your body posture right now, and invite an awareness of that solar plexus center. Is there heat or energy, a knotted feeling, an emotion? Just notice.

Many of us have been underrepresented or underserved by our internal power centers. We may need core-strengthening practices. You can draw from a growing firmness as you practice strengthening the core of your body through physical exercise. You could also explore metaphorical energy strengthening, like the following practice:

> Begin by listing four or five of the most prominent obstacles in your path, including external barriers as well as any pesky internal ones you'd like to play with. If you have a person who'd be willing to help you with this exercise, that's ideal. You may use pillows or blankets or a mattress or even a wall as a somewhat less interactive prop if you don't. Ask your helper to represent the first of the obstacles (for instance, "I just don't have the talent," or "Publishing is dead!") and to stand in your way as you aim toward your big dream, only moving aside when it becomes convinced that you have overcome that obstacle. You may persuade or yell or reason, you may push physically, you may wheedle or seduce, but you must press through the barrier in order to....encounter the next one! Practice this until you've successfully met and bested every obstacle you listed. Pat yourself firmly on your back or do a Victory Dance. Notice the strength you have generated. Notice how any of these obstacles look to you now. Notice how this core strength can be your ally. Write about it if you want to.

Wisdom and Sensitivity: The Gut Sense

Perceptions and appetites are conveyed to the brain from the gut twice as quickly as the blink of an eye, via the gut sense, the intuitive connection between belly and brain, a powerful ally in our writing lives.

Our friend Buddy Wakefield, poet and three-time world champion of spoken word performance and a self-described obsessive editor of his own work, advises that when we read our work aloud, we listen internally for the "stomach drop," a signal that maybe we've gotten lazy with a word or missed a chance to keep the energy of the piece charged and alive. Stop there, he says, and dive in.

The pit of your stomach. The feeling of walking into a building and knowing that something is wrong there. Gut sense. The sense on meeting someone that you've seen them, known them before. The great sorrow you feel from a poem you don't even understand intellectually. A sucker punch to the gut.

While intuition can be a powerful ally to writers, many sensitive people have learned to guard against the possibility of the sucker punch. In favor of comfort and calm, many of us step back from the vulnerable edge where living fully and writing powerfully must stand. If you're committed to writing, you will — if you haven't already — see and feel that vulnerable edge. You will — if you haven't already — feel the heat and know there is fire ahead.

Please keep writing. There is also light in the fire.

Wide Open Writing editorial staffer Nikki Kallio puts it this way, "You learn that you can't avoid the dark, and in fact, it's long past time to seek it out. You learn that sometimes pain is least painful when you crawl inside it, become it, find its smallest origin, and expand inside it until it bursts. To look under the bed and say, hello, monster, come out and play. You begin to see the beauty in the whole, to understand that painters seek the right kind of light not for the light itself but for the play of light and

dark together."

Let's work with this play of darkness and light now, knowing that after this next writing exercise, we'll offer a few tips on managing the anxiety of living on the edge.

> **Go to the most challenging (vulnerable, scary, difficult) place in your writing project, and write the thing you do not want to write.** *If you don't have a project now, chances are you still have something you do not want to write. Write it anyway. Leap into the fire. Write for 30 minutes to leave it all on the page.*

When you've completed your 30-minute write, take a break for juice or tea or coffee and fresh air, and then come back to read your piece aloud. Do your very best to access kindness, compassion, and permission for this sensitive being who dared to bring forth her or his tender, raging, fierce, wounded truth, who stepped forth "determined to save the only life (it) could save"(Mary Oliver).

Is it possible that writing the thing you did not want to write made space inside for what you *do* want to write next?

The gut will keep us honest, and honesty of that kind is our tether to good writing. It's not the whole shebang: Skill and craft will come along to sweep up and beautify, and they will sculpt it for others to see what you are seeing and make it shine. But if you are traveling into the fertile darkness and keeping your wits about you, and if you are returning from the darkness having salvaged truth and some measure of radiance, you are doing the real work of the writer in the world.

Writing is necessarily an act of courage, and anxiety accompanies every act of courage. Think about practicing one or two of the following methods if your gut tells you that you're struggling:

Breathing: Pause for a count of three at the top of the inhale and at the bottom of the exhale, experiencing both fullness and stillness. That pause at the bottom of the exhale in particular signals calm. All is well.

Thinking: We are capable of so much more power concerning our thoughts than we know. Grow your relationship to this power and watch yourself become a navigational pro.

> *Think useful thoughts:* Spend more time with thoughts you would like to cultivate than with the ones that don't help.
>
> *Dis-identify from your writing:* "I am not my writing" can help when presenting our work to others and to ourselves.
>
> *Get better at appraising the situation:* Is this situation actually dangerous?
>
> *Give anxious thoughts a little breathing room:* 10 minutes is enough.

Discharging: Sometimes screaming in your car is called for. Sometimes pounding on a pillow or kicking your feet, or shaking all over. Discharge offers release from what holds you down.

Writing: Trust that the process you've committed to is also committed to you. Grow in patience: Your writing will give you the answers you seek.

15
Connection and Support

"In the beginning is Relation."

— Martin Buber

"We believe that getting away and connecting to nature and ourselves is central to the creative process. In this place of respite, we find our deeper truths." This quote from the Wide Open Writing website speaks a truth we firmly believe: Disconnecting to connect makes for powerful magic. We break away from the routines that form 'regular' life to come into silence and natural beauty, where we begin again or for the first time to hear our own voices. And as we connect with our senses and witness the beginnings of transformation in our writing, we're able to more authentically, powerfully and often playfully connect with one another. We speak in poetry and limerick and essay and novella and find our words echoed by others to whom we show facets of our beings we had not previously shown even to ourselves. It's a blast. It's almost impossible to leave.

A Wide Open Writing retreat in Tuscany in the light of late summer cannot be beat. But until you come to find us in that little hamlet of San Donato outside of the "medieval Manhattan" of San Gimignano, until the circumstances of your life allow that luxurious necessity, we want to help you develop your network of supportive connections right where you are.

First things first: *Cultivate a connection with yourself.* Morning pages. Play dates. The practices of yoga and meditation. Alone time. Regularity and ritual in your writing practice. Whatever it takes.

Wherever you have put yourself to write, writing is almost always a solitary activity. Maya

Angelou rented hotel rooms where all decorations had been removed and made herself stay there with only the decor of her internal spaces for inspiration. I wrote much of this book on a makeshift desk in a cabin 100 yards from my home where almost nothing, even electricity, could serve as distraction. When we strip the externals to their smooth essentials, whether in woodland cabin or corner Starbucks, we find we've created the space we can then begin to fill with character and setting and story.

Having found ourselves with ourselves now, having put on our writing pants and our writing music, having closed the internet connection and bowed to our altars, having done whatever it takes to get to that writing chair, what comes next?

Whether we're alone in the chair or sitting with a circle of fellow travelers, creativity is always about connection. Connecting memory with intention in creating memoir. Singing together with another, harmony rising from the space between. Writing as a way of connecting your understanding of your mother's childhood with an imagined child of a different culture. Hearing in the story of a friend a hint of something that resonates deep in your belly. Connection with ourselves. With nature. With one another. Connection between thoughts and feelings and body sensations. Connection with the senses. Connection with the divine.

> **Try this exploration of connection as creative inspiration.**
>
> **Choose a published poem (preferably longer than a haiku and shorter than TS Eliot's Four Quartets), one you don't know well but like the sound of, and read it aloud. Now close the book or the laptop and write that poem for yourself.**

Unless your photographic memory is perfect, the new poem — filtered through your senses and your fingers — will be your own, created by you in connection with this beloved poet. You may find juicy new ideas flowing from the simple exercise of blatantly copying another writer only to find that you really can't do it! Because you are a born creator.

Creativity responds to the surprise of an invitation to make new neural pathways. This, of course, is another reason we've come on this retreat together. When we breathe different smells in the air, hear other languages, see colors that are not the colors of our home environments, our sensoria come alive. And although it's not Tuscany, we can approximate this awakening at home in enough ways that we might decide never to travel again!

I went to a songwriting workshop where participants were asked to draw three pieces of paper from a hat and create a song from the prompts those words presented. I pulled *aeronautics*, *home*, and *recycle*, which initially seemed to me unlikely to produce anything at all from my writer self, but which in fact turned into a lovely little song. Even when faced with the presence of seemingly random words, our synapses long to connect with one another!

> **If you like the sound of the three words in the preceding paragraph, write your own song or poem or essay from the surprise of their encounter. Then, take this further. Put dozens of words in a hat or ask someone to gift you with words they'd like to prompt you with, and when your creative vessel feels a bit low, pull out three words and watch them make a connection with one another on the page.**

Buddy Wakefield keeps a list of Big Ideas made up of random Tweets and profound thoughts and phrases he's composed that didn't yet find their way into poems. He periodically mines this list to make new poems directly from those lines, poems which form at the *points of connection* among the words and phrases. We've noticed that the files of leftovers we keep in the computer for phrases we couldn't bear to kill are remarkably intuitively consistent, an internal reliability that defies reason but embraces creativity.

When you've had enough of connecting with your internal world, please remember that you are a child of the Earth and that she is here offering her lap to you. Our connections with the world who bears us have frayed and shredded over the centuries since dragons and fairies and nature spirits spoke to us loudly and convincingly, but we can listen to her whispers. She is still here in all her patient strength, and we can — in fact, we must — always come home.

> **Take some time in forest-bathing, opening your senses to every sight and sound and smell and touch and taste. When you feel lost or stuck with a piece of writing, go outside. Take a walk and ask your questions to the world around you. Pay attention. When you come home, tell a story of what you've noticed there.**

We can't emphasize enough the importance of this simple act of connection, of simultaneously turning toward our inner worlds and our natural world and listening there for the sound of wings, for the rhythm of the seasons, the rise and fall of inspiration and contemplation, of sun and moon. Maybe you'll discover again that you are not *on* the earth but that you *are* the earth, given a voice.

Connection with ourselves. Connection to our roots in the earth. And of huge importance, connection with *one another*, people "with whom we can share the counsels of the heart and speak a language of the heart." (Edward Sellner)

If we are not One, we are at least, as indigenous people have long known, all relations; and we are reminded of this at every turn. In the year 2020, smoke from devastating fires in California and Oregon clouded skies all the way to Maine and as far away as Europe. The internet links us all in viral connection at still unimaginable speeds. And yet, COVID-19 had the capacity to stop and transform the entire human world as we knew it. We lost touch, literally, with one another. We lived in bubbles, sometimes made up of one or two people. And still we found ways, however virtual, to connect, because this is who we are. Even if writing is done alone, and even among the most introverted of writers, our need for one another is unarguable.

Wide Open Writing retreats begin, as you might imagine, in awkwardness and anticipation (and sometimes dread!). Then each retreat evolves into its version of what we've come to call sacred community. We believe you'd recognize the particular qualities of reverence and play, vulnerability and power, expansion and depth, that attend us when we gather with intention and integrity. These are the qualities we'd love for you to look for in your communities.

> **Reflect on the core beings in your life. Consider making a drawing or a map of their importance and their closeness or distance to you.** *For instance, you might represent a beloved partner by a large circle at the center of your page and your life. A dear friend who has grown distant might be a smaller circle or a triangle at the far corner of your page. Your dog. Your children. Your parents, living or in the spirit world. Ancestors from your bloodline and witnesses from traditions you respect. Buddha. Ruth Bader Ginsburg. Black Elk. Martin Luther King Jr. Writers you love. Toni Morrison. Rumi. Let them all come to the page, and once they've arrived, notice what you see there. A crowd? A sparseness? If you sense very few people circling you there and you'd like more, notice that. And notice the quality of these relationships. Are they ones that support the whole creative authenticity you seek?*

Sometimes our core communities need strengthening. The work of the writer is difficult and brave. We look for other writers in the flesh who will understand and support our fledging and our flight. We seek out witnesses to our sorrow and our delight. We stand naked in front of others, hoping that the mirror they reflect will be kind as well as genuine. We bring vulnerability and hope that we may try again to love as if for the first time. We have already been hurt. We have all known the pain of rejection or of being unwelcome or undervalued. Each time, we pray that this time it will not happen.

We're devoted to creating and maintaining spaces where we expand our trust in ourselves and others. In addition to the retreats that may call to you, our dream is to help create writing groups in towns worldwide, and in online communities for those who don't have access to other writers where they are. And wherever we are, you are welcome to join in this experiment in authentic and joyful creativity.

When WOW first began to meet together in Italy, we were surprised to hear many writers speaking of the negative, even traumatic, experiences they'd had in previous group and retreat experiences. In truth, though, we were both surprised and unsurprised. Every one of us could summon up a story of our own of having been ambushed by well-intentioned criticism or careless advice. Many of us have been silenced by the chilling experience of bringing a newly birthed piece of writing into the icy space of a "critique" group or an encounter with an envious friend. We spoke in Chapter Fourteen about strengthening the core, and those practices will serve you well when you need them. But we would also like to suggest that if you want to generate new work or expand awareness of your creativity and your individual voice, bringing that vulnerable new work to others

in the "workshopping" format may not *initially* serve you best. Critique is not the best response to new writing.

We have great respect for creatives, and respect mixed with caution for the academic models that meet and greet newly generated writing with harsh critique. We've come to understand the distribution of labor inside each of us between writer and editor, each with clear tasks of their own. Similarly, we are wise to realize that writing groups and editing groups, while both may be valuable, are not the same.

Creativity does not like to be fenced in. Theories of learning based on calling attention to what isn't working come primarily from a principle of *containment*, as though removing the awkward words from a piece of writing will make it great. This is partly true. Editing is terrific fun, like vacuuming and cleaning counters and polishing furniture. But first, there have to be plush carpets and granite counters and 18th-century armoires to shine. First, there has to be writing that is alive. For this, we need fields without fences, rooms without walls, meetings with people who are reliably affirmative, generative, and wildly expansive. We need to cultivate shame-free zones and to maintain those zones against any countervailing winds of suppression in the guise of critical intelligence.

Expansion and generativity, once cultivated, continue to ripple out. After our retreats, participants stay in touch with one another, seek guidance from each other, share silliness and profundity, plan and keep reunion dates. We couldn't ask for anything more.

We need one another, yet we need to care for ourselves enough to let only supportive humans have access to the core courage of our creative lives.

In addition to growing the relationship you have with yourself as beloved, as creator, as trustworthy companion, **with which open-minded and open-hearted beings can you share your writing?** Bring all your insights from previous chapters to this question and take a few minutes to think about how you might expand any sparsely populated creative community of which you're a part, or how to create a community where there may have been none. How might you connect with others of your courageous and far-flung tribe? Writing opportunities, including online Wide Open Writing groups, do exist! Know that you are far from alone, and know that connections of the juiciest sort can sustain us through even the most difficult moments of our writing journeys.

Where to find these connections? No standardized criteria exist to define what will be the most exciting and nourishing support group for you, but some broad distinctions may help. Are you looking for a *generative writing group* of the sort we outline in this book? Consider these resources, all with an online presence: Wide Open Writing. Gateless Writing, founded by Suzanne Kingsbury. MeetUp writing groups in your local area. Zona Rosa, the brainchild of Rosemary Daniell. Or consider forming your own group, perhaps using the chapters of this book as structure.

If you're looking for a group that will hold and support you as you commit to a writing project, you may need to dig deeper. Have you met anyone whose writing you love and whose judgment you appreciate? Could you ask them to form a group with you? Two participants from a WOW retreat in Mexico continue to offer feedback and suggestions to one another on their projects three years later. Are local resources available through writing centers or through MeetUp? In Maine where WOW is headquartered, Maine Writers and Publishers Association (MWPA) sponsors a number of workshops and courses from which new writing alliances arise; similar connections are available in many other states. Given that we're sensitive beings and that not all group settings will be right for any one of us, this step may not be an easy one. Ask around. Ask your friends. Ask us. Don't give up.

16
Manifestation and Celebration

"Ask for what you want and be prepared to get it."

— Maya Angelou

Our time together in this retreat builds on the invitation to open mind, heart, movement, spirit, memory, voice, and connection to a writing world of wonders and a lifetime of possibility. We believe that wide openness is truly the key to living well and writing well. Even more audaciously, we believe in the tremendous power of creative expression in healing ourselves, our relationships, and our broken world. That "audacious hope" Barack Obama speaks of keeps us alive, and we have every hope that it is already doing the same for you.

So, let's bring it all together here in some final exercises.

We've focused on expanding channels to creative genius. Now that we've written for a while together, we're ready to talk a bit more about fine-tuning our work and to offer some lively inspirations in that direction.

Imagine the massive block of marble Michelangelo brings into his studio. Imagine that in the marble, he begins to see the shape of David, the Biblical human hero to be honored in what will become possibly the world's greatest sculpture. Imagine the first sculpting strike of his chisel.

Did you know that the 25-foot block of marble Michelangelo was given to work with had been rejected by at least two other prominent sculptors of the time for its imperfections and its potential structural weaknesses? Did he know that? He, a human no more perfect than any one of us, nonetheless created that breathtaking sculpture out of imperfect marble, at least in part because he could see with fresh eyes. The imperfections of both stone and artist do not to this day detract at all from the stunning beauty of the work that emerged.

In the work you've done throughout this book, we imagine there are also imperfections and structural weaknesses. But might you look with the fresh eyes of Michelangelo at the beauty that lives inside the stone? That's what fine-tuning is all about. And we think that's truly exciting.

On the final afternoon of our Tuscany retreat, we dress up a bit and gather under the chestnut tree at the edge of the lawn, golden hills to the west offering their soft backdrop, and we stage a formal reading. We invite participants and staff to read something they've worked on a bit. We get to listen on that Thursday evening to the partially or entirely polished works we may have encountered earlier in the week as rough chunks of marble. In this ceremony, we meet ourselves even more fully as writers, emergent.

> For one of our final exercises of this retreat-in-a-book, we'd like to invite you to choose one of the pieces you've written during the retreat and to play with editing that piece for a reading. We'll give you some ideas for exciting strategies to try, and while there may be more ideas here than you'll ever use, we invite you to apply at least two of them to the piece. Try more if you like. Try them all, as each has a gem of creativity contained within. You may think of these exercises as your final explorations - for now - in the practice of generative writing, and as the beginning of refining your work.

1. *Add a smell.* Smell is our most primitive sense. We know in our viscera the power of its information.
2. *Add as many senses as you possibly can.*
3. *Cut out half the words.* Don't cheat. Half the words. It will be easy at first. Extra adjectives. All adverbs. Meanders that don't serve. It will get more demanding, and that in itself is interesting.
4. In the words of Buddy Wakefield, *"turn your cliches into better people!"* Look for the cliches, and dive in there to take the metaphor out farther, toward words and phrases that are more vivid or more intense, but not so far that you lose the reader.
5. *Write the piece again, from a different point of view.* Another character. Another voice, not I but she. Not he but you. Notice the differences.
6. *Blow the piece open by starting somewhere else.* Start with your last sentence, for instance, or your fifth.
7. *Have someone else read the work out loud.* How does it sound? Does the rhythm work? Do the sentences sing?
8. After you've read the piece out loud, ask yourself, *"What is the question this piece of work is addressing?"* In Dulcie's thesis manuscript, which would come to be called Crooked Love, she recognized that it addressed the questions, "What is this thing we call love? Can we love someone who hurts us deeply? Can we love when we are wounded? Is all love crooked

in some way, born from the healing of previous wounds?"

Her next step in editing was to read through again and see if she had indeed answered these questions.

Now, it's time for your reading. You may want to dress up a bit or a lot. Consider the suggestion that you share your most vulnerable self with people who will treat you with care. You may want to ask someone to attend your reading. Stand up to read. Visualize the eager audience. Show them what you've got. Show yourself what you've got. Accept the applause with as much grace as possible. And when you've finished, please pat yourself on the back or hug yourself.

Be watchful for the voices of internal or external doubters, as this is a moment when they may want to give you their "helpful" advice. Consider this an opportunity to bow to them and remind them you don't need their help during a reading and that you'd like to fully enjoy this moment of manifestation. You have moved from where you were — inchoate images, a sense of a story you wanted to tell, an idea for memoir, curiosity about what kind of writer you might be — through *all* the steps involved in actually producing a piece of writing and presenting it to the world.

CONGRATULATIONS!

We approach the closing hours of our retreat together. We have come to Thursday evening, our minibus will pull up on the bricked drive on Friday morning, and rolling suitcases will clatter down the stairs and along the scented paths. We'll get ready to pile in for the drive to Florence, where we'll say goodbye. Imagine all the feelings that might accompany your preparation to leave this magical place and time. Imagine that your "real world" begins to whisper its way into your thoughts as you face what comes next: Travel, companions to meet at train stations, family, work, chores, the future.

And now, please pause. Don't leave yet. We're going to take some time to notice what we've accomplished. We're going to celebrate, because without celebration, mastery is incomplete. Without celebration, every accomplishment diminishes.

Maybe you're done. You're tempted to close this book now and move on to the next thing. Perhaps you've noticed that this is a moment where discomfort arises for you. If you typically tend to minimize the pluses and maximize the minuses of your days and your ways, may we suggest that this will have to change? That it is already changing? If you are going to live your inspirations, your dreams, your heart's desires, if you are going to claim the authentic creativity that is at your very essence, if you are going to move beyond what's in the way of bringing your voice out in the world, please do not contract at this very last moment into caution and self-consciousness.

What would please your inner writer?

Could you find or buy something for her or him that represents your wildly successful completion of the retreat? Our inner artists like to be honored. Could you host a party? We want to be seen, even if we're shy. Could you dance like crazy, dancing on the doubts as well as the exultations? Could you bow to yourself with real respect? Our inner artists are children, some say, and they like all the things we enjoyed as children: They want to be loved, they like to play and dance and get presents, things that are their very own. They are feeling-full and need their feelings to be understood. The more you honor your writer, the more s/he will show him or herself to you. That's neuroanatomy as well as common sense. The more you call on him, the more intelligent and alive he will be. The more fun she has, the more liveliness she'll bring to you. Take some time to give your writer good juju, and that's what your writer will give you in return.

Many writers agree that it's the process and not the product of writing itself that is most rewarding. We hope it's true for you that you find deep and sustaining joy in the expansive process of writing itself. We hope you write what is genuine and that you rejoice in the growing skill with which you express your truth.

We hope you carve works of great beauty from the initial imperfections of your writing and your being. We believe in manifestation. We believe in the products and the process of writing, and we think more of us need to be seen, read, and understood. We know there's something about a physical book written by a physical person that is immensely satisfying to hold and to share. We are constant cheerleaders for making work that can be seen. Practice manifestation. Practice abundance.

And enjoy your experience with the wealth that follows.

As a teenager living upstairs from his parents' dry-cleaning business, Jim Carrey drew for himself a check for twelve million dollars and dated it ten years in the future. Day after day, he would drive up to the Hollywood Hills, survey the city below him, and look at that check. Ten years later, in the year written on his check, he signed a contract for twelve million dollars for his part in *Ace Ventura, Pet Detective*. Manifestation and literal wealth.

> **Take a few moments to re-visit the visualization exercise in Chapter 8 and let it grow now with all you've created and discovered in the course of this book.** Let yourself see the details of success as you envision it. Let yourself smell it and hear it and taste it and touch it, the pleasurable weight of the book, the smile of the child who reads your story, the sound of applause, the peace in your heart. Notice the wealth of this vision. Let it be vivid in the way that a story you have wanted to tell is already alive, waiting only for your wide-open attention, your faith, and your perseverance.
>
> In the spirit of remembering what you've accomplished here, please find a nice piece of stationery and an envelope. **Write a letter to yourself with whatever is in your heart now.** Put it in an envelope, seal the envelope, and do one of these several things: Give it to a friend with the request that they mail it to you at just the right time. Hide it somewhere where you'll see it in several months (when you change the smoke alarm or when you put summer clothes away or when you register your car). Or let it sit on your altar or in your writing space until you determine the time is right and necessary for opening the letter.

Close your eyes and listen for a moment to words others in the group might say about your writing as they've experienced it during the retreat. Can you hear whispers of those voices and what they might be saying about your writing? Perhaps there's a phrase that stays with you from a piece you wrote, a moment during the work of this book when you noticed that you liked how lyrical or succinct, how clear or authentic, how musical or strong your writing sounded to you. Let those moments drift back to you and "hear" them as they sink into your heart. Believe them. Write them down.

> **Is there one commitment you'd like to make to yourself about how you will live when you leave this retreat?** *Is there one thread of devotion and discipline you'll carry with you or one quality of mind you'd like to make your own? What specifically would you like to promise to your writer self? And how will s/he help you in your life? Take a few minutes to write from this prompt and, as we've learned to do, read this aloud, listening for what rings true.*

Your experience here has changed you. Please do not forget this or minimize its import. We will go from this place, but this place will not go from us. And neither will we entirely leave behind the experience of giving ourselves this gift of time and attention and intention.

Remember this: The cells of your body are transformed by the feelings you have felt and the thoughts you have thought, by the words you have written and read. Know that you bring all of this wealth with you to your next chapter. The writer in you will continue to be enriched by your experiences of our retreat together, as will all the other parts of you. They will thank you for your attention to their expansion.

And what comes next?

Write on. We'd love to see you in person at any of our Wide Open Writing retreats when that calls to you.

Thank you.

> *Only what we manage to do*
>   *lasts, what love sculpts from us:*
> *but what I count...*
> *are those moments*
> *wide open when I know clearly*
> *who I am, who you are, what we*
> *do, a marigold, an oakleaf, a meteor,*
> *with all my senses hungry and filled*
> *at once like a pitcher with light."*
> — Marge Piercy

APPENDICES

APPENDIX A. Additional Prompts

Take the title of a poem you love and use that title as inspiration for your writing.

Write a description of your fear, its color, its smell, where it lives in your body. What is most likely to get it going, and how do you act when you're afraid? Personify it. Animate it. Tell a story of a time when this fear had a hold on you.

Write about a challenging thing that happened in your life. Before you start writing, close your eyes, and put yourself there. Smell it, listen in, look around, feel for temperature and time of day, locate it in terms of what else was occurring at the time. Don't worry about picking just the right thing, but instead choose the first thing that pops into your mind.

Write about something that looked like a bad thing but turned out to be a good thing.

Write about a part of yourself as a character you like. Write about a part of yourself as a character you don't like. Create a scene where they are doing something together.

Who would you be without your wound?

What is your relationship to softness? To grit?

Where do you come from?

APPENDIX B. Readings

Bell, Susan. *The Artful Edit: On the Practice of Editing Yourself*. W. W. Norton & Company, 2008. A great companion for the editing process - essays, stories, quotes on the art of revising and polishing our work.

Cameron, Julia. *The Artist's Way*. Pan Macmillan, 1995. The classic book on recovering creativity and well worth reading, particularly for the introduction of Morning Pages and Artist Dates.

Gilbert, Elizabeth. *Big Magic*. Penguin, 2015. Not a book about how to write so much as a book about how to dream big and live that life you dream about. Nonetheless there are plenty of writing stories to think on as well.

Goldberg, Natalie. *Writing Down the Bones*. Shambhala Publications, 2016. Writing practice as spiritual practice is the goal, working toward writing the "essential awake speech of the mind." When she first wrote this book in 1985 she "didn't realize (she) was breaking the paradigm of how writing was understood and taught in this country."

Howe, Marie. *What the Living Do: Poems*. W. W. Norton & Company, 1999. This collection explores the poetry of childhood growing into adulthood and how we carry loss along with us. Howe wrote the title poem in the form of a letter to her younger brother who died of AIDS in the 1980s. "Poetry holds the knowledge that we are alive and that we know we're going to die," says Howe. "The most mysterious aspect of being alive might be that—and poetry knows that." Howe shows us what bright lights of beauty there are in the minutiae of everyday life.

King, Stephen. *On Writing*. Hachette UK, 2001. Even if you're not a fan of King's books, you will appreciate this one. Part writer's memoir, part "what I've learned so far," part instruction manual in which every writer will find something of value.

Kiteley, Brian. *3 AM Epiphany*. Penguin, 2005. Stuck? Uninspired? So what! Kiteley says in this book of writing exercises. Get your butt in a chair and begin, again and again. Like athletes, musicians, and car mechanics, writers get better at writing with practice. With chapters examining point of view, characters and ways of seeing, thought and emotion, internal structures, and a lot more, Kiteley, a creative fiction instructor and writer, has a goal in The 3 a.m. Epiphany "to teach writers how to let their fiction find itself."

Lamott, Anne. *Bird by Bird*. Anchor, 2007. Anne Lamott uses a story from her childhood to build a structure for stepping into the story you want to write - taking it an idea at a time, eating a bite at a time, drawing one bird at a time. The originator of the exhortation to write "the Shitty First Draft" as a way to let the whole thing reveal itself without the editor getting in the way, Lamott captures our hearts as well as our pens with her humor and her humility.

Lerner, Betsy. *The Forest for the Trees*. Riverhead Books (Hardcover), 2000. A veteran of the publishing industry, Lerner dissects the working relationship between agent, editor, and writer into insightful nuggets of knowledge. This gem guides the writer through writing stalls, discipline, and what happens next once the work is done.

Paintner, Christine Valters. *The Artist's Rule*. Ave Maria Press, 2011. A lovely book of practices for those who identify or would like to identify as both artists and contemplatives, incorporated in a twelve-week journey.

Pressfield, Steven. *The War of Art*. Black Irish Entertainment LLC, 2002. This very widely read book is a bit stern in its tone, and that can feel helpful - its best use is as a procrastination-buster and on how to move from amateur to professional.

Prose, Francine. *Reading Like a Writer*. Union Books, 2012. Francine Prose, novelist, short story writer, and essayist, maintains you can't write well if you don't read well. Taking the time to discover the many layers of meaning in well-written books helps the novice or advanced writer improve their work. This book breaks the page down from recognizing rhythmic paragraphs to using the perfect word.

Sanders, Scott Russell. *Writing From the Center*. Musings from a writer and professor of writing on the importance of place, of literally knowing our place on the planet, and then coming from that deeply rooted place in our writing. What is the nature of the soil underneath our feet? What is the story this place wants to tell?

Shaughnessy, Susan. *Walking on Alligators*. Harper Collins, 1993. Concise, daily meditations for writers seeking a little creative boost to their writing practice — offers encouragement & ways to help your psyche stay on track.

Ueland, Brenda. *If You Want to Write*. 1987. Originally published in 1938 and revised in 1983, this book on writing is still thought by many to be the most valuable read if you want to be a better writer. Ueland's vision, "Everybody is Talented, Original and Has Something Important to Say," titles one of the most impressive chapters, and it is from here that she unfolds her ideas on how to bring your unique genius onto the page.

Winokur, Jon. *Advice to Writers*. Vintage, 2010. Quotes of all sorts from writers of all kinds on many of the obvious aspects of being and becoming a writer. If there is a thought about writing that seems to you convincing, there is both a quote to support that and another to refute it entirely.

Wood, Monica. *Pocket Muse*. Writer's Digest Books, 2002. Dulcie used this book to help build her first class, "Memoir to Fiction: Making It Up To Make It Real." Filled with short zingers and prompts, scenarios and characters, Wood generously lays out methods to get at the secrets that hide between the lines you've already written as well as the ones you haven't written yet.

APPENDIX C
Sample WOW Retreat Schedules

Tuscany
Wide Open Writing
A Retreat for the Senses
Fattoria Voltrona, Tuscany
September 1st - 6th, 2019

Dearest Writers,

Well well well. Welcome. Benvenuti.

Here you are. Reading this in Tuscany, surrounded by the nature you've been dreaming about since your heart first tugged you toward this space, this landscape. Along with your comfy shoes, favorite pen and p.j.s, perhaps you have brought with you some hopes, dreams and wishes for yourself on this journey. Through writing, shared meals, morning meditation (and more!) it is our desire to fill your senses and help you birth those yearnings and dreams. Along with the sheer joy of your time here, we want to be part of an experience where you identify the things you need in your life on a daily basis in order to stay true to your creative self and your work.

Maybe you are here because you want to see what this is all about, this part of yourself who wants to write. Maybe you're here because you need time away from the day to day. Maybe you're here because you'd like to write something other than what you've been working on. Or perhaps you're here to complete something in its entirety – a poem, a short story, a script or a full eight hours' worth of sleep. Whatever your reason, we encourage you to embrace it, honor it and then let it go. Beyond your own reasons for coming you've also come here for reasons that are rooted at the soul-level, not visible to the conscious mind. Congratulate yourself for answering the call. And know that now, it's just time to let it flow, jive and dance. Enjoy.

Be good to yourself while you're here. Listen to what's going on and know that only you can give yourself what you need – whether that's a game of cards, a hot shower, a long walk alone or a nap. Take this ride for what it is – everything you wanted, nothing like you expected – and trust that you have been guided. Take it easy and be gentle with yourself. Participate in this schedule as much or as little as you choose. And don't be afraid to write your heart out.

Thank you for joining us. We're so glad you're here.

With love,

Dulcie, Nancy, Nikki, Pam and Vanessa

And I wondered, with mounting anxiety, 'What am I supposed to do here? What am I supposed to think?'

Alain de Botton, *The Art of Travel*

Sunday, September 1st - I Am Here Now
1pm	Arrive at the farm for lunch
5-7pm	Opening session - bring something to write with and your poem/quote/prayer to share
7:15pm	Dinner

Monday, September 2nd - Body as Messenger
8:00am - 9:00am	Optional Morning Yoga with Nancy
9:00am - 10:00am	Breakfast in Silence
10:30am - 12:00pm	Morning session: Body as Messenger
15 min break	
12:15 - 12:30pm	The Mirror: Praise and Criticism
1pm	Lunch (pranzo) followed by free time - laze by the pools, hike, nap, write, play, fish, write, write, write. Appointments available for individual sessions and Thai massage.
5-7pm	Evening session
7:15pm	Dinner

Stand still. The trees ahead and bushes beside you
Are not lost. Wherever you are is called Here,
And you must treat it as a powerful stranger,
Must ask permission to know it and be known.
 — *Lost* by David Wagoner, from *Collected Poems 1956-1976*

Tuesday, September 3rd - Body as Place
8:00am - 9:00am	Optional Morning Yoga with Nancy
9:00am - 10:00am	Breakfast in Silence
10:30-12:30pm	Morning session: Body as Place
1:00pm - 2:00pm	Lunch (pranzo) followed by free time - laze by the pools, hike, nap, write, play, fish, write, write, write. Appointments available for individual sessions and Thai massage.
5:00pm -7:00pm	Evening session
7:15pm - 8:30pm	Dinner
8:30pm	Talent(less) Night

"I took a deep breath and listened to the old brag of my heart. I am, I am, I am."

9:00 - 10:00am	Morning session (please bring your bag and key to the reception prior to group.
10:00am	Depart
12:00pm	Arrive at Florence airport

Borestone Mountain Retreat
Writing the Wild
July 27-31, 2017

"Nature is actually the silent witness of intuition."
— Malidoma Some, Leader of the Dagara People

Thursday, July 27th

1pm	Meet at parking lot
2pm	Arrive at the lodge, Welcome and Orientation, Get settled in rooms, unpack, swim, play, explore
6pm	Dinner
7pm	After-dinner gathering (bring a quote/poem/prayer to read)

Friday, July 28th

7-8am	Optional morning yoga (all levels) led by Nancy
8-9am	Breakfast in silence
10am-12pm	Writing Session 1 – Connecting the Writer to her Story
12:30-1:30	Lunch
1:30-3:30pm	Free time
3:30-5:30pm	Afternoon Writing Session – Connecting to Emotions, led by Nikki Kallio

As we begin to absorb the magic of our surroundings and feel the magic growing within us, we will tap into that energy to either develop an old story or conjure a new one. Nikki will lead us through an exercise using oracle/picture cards to facilitate the drawing out of emotions and letting them flow onto the page.

6-7pm	Dinner
Evening	Free

Saturday, July 29th

7-8am	Optional morning yoga (all levels)
8-9am	Breakfast in silence
10-12pm	Writing Session 2 – Growing and Fueling the Story
12:30-1:30pm	Lunch
1:30-3:30	Free time
3:30-5:30	Dance/Journey with Nancy Coleman

Because we are the wild, our bodies can lead us directly to the truths we seek. We gather in this guided afternoon workshop to awaken, embody, immerse, express, release and celebrate, and then to write. No level of "dance" proficienty is expected, and every body is the perfect body for this experience.

6-7pm	Dinner
7pm	Reading

Listen to the wind, it speaks. Listen to silence, it speaks. Listen to your heart, it knows.

— Native American proverb

Sunday, July 30th

7-8am	Optional morning yoga (all levels)
8-9am	Breakfast in silence
10-12pm	Writing session #3 – The Climax
12:30-1:30	Lunch
1:30-3:30pm	Free time
3:30-5:30pm	Painting Truth and Questions, with Mary Brooking
6-7pm	Dinner
7pm	TBD

Monday, July 31st

7-8am	Optional morning yoga (all levels)
8-9am	Breakfast in silence
9:30am	Closing session – Where will I go from here?
11:00am	Depart

ACKNOWLEDGMENTS

Ubuntu: I am because we are.

I'd like to honor COVID-19, without whom I doubt this book could have been written, and with whose devastating help we've learned about patience, perseverance, radical acceptance, and adaptation, as well as about the power of our own maxim: Keep writing.

To Dulcie Witman and Regina Tingle, who started the big foolish project we call Wide Open Writing, and in particular to Dulcie, who inspires us again and again with her vision and her vital energy, even when she'd rather be writing her own book! To Pam Dumlao, Jolly Goins, Robin Gaines, Nikki Kallio, Vanessa Dunleavy, and Eline van Wieren, the once and future WOW Mermaids, my gratitude for who you are goes on forever. To the hundreds of participants who've graced Wide Open Writing retreats over the years, vivid memories of each of you are woven into the language and philosophy of the book. You are the Why.

To the writing teachers whose insight and skill made a writer out of a wannabe, I humbly thank Joan Hunter and Suzanne Kingsbury, whose wisdom, optimism and courage I draw on daily. Significant thanks as well to a host of teachers over the years, and to the generous guest speakers who've graced our WOW membership series in 2020-21. To Kim Brown of Minerva Rising Press, who guided this book and its author from draft to finished manuscript with clarity, directness and kindness, you rock. I don't know how you do it, but I'm so grateful that you do.

To my dear friends, writers and non-writers alike, thank you for every word of advice and nod of understanding and grace of space you've had to make for this effort to come to fruition. And finally, a deep bow of gratitude for the support of my two remaining brothers: John, for fiercely believing in what we're doing; and Steve, for the ongoing inspiration for this book, thank you. I love you.

This book emerges from the collective imagination of the Wide Open Writing team. I am its scribe, responsible for any missteps or errors in judgment, and endlessly grateful to the team for any brilliance that shines through.

NANCY COLEMAN

Nancy Coleman is a writer of songs, poetry, essays, creative nonfiction, and two full-length fiction manuscripts, *I See My Light Come Shining*, and *From Our Birth*, in consideration for publication. Her work has been published in The Sun, Minerva Rising, and in the compilation, Maine Voices.

Nancy has been a practicing psychologist for more than thirty years, earning her PhD from Columbia University. She's studied mindfulness, body-mind integrative practices, yoga and EMDR. She's fascinated by how new discoveries in the science of psychology weave together with ancient Eastern wisdom to inform our journeys to creativity and health.

Nancy has two grown children. Along with her partner Dulcie, she lives by a river in Maine, in a garden in Florida, in a camper traveling the country, and at every writing retreat offered by WOW.

www.ingramcontent.com/pod-product-compliance
Lightning Source LLC
Chambersburg PA
CBHW060942170426
43196CB00022B/2960